THE WORSHIP WORKSHOP

THE Worship WORKSHOP

CREATIVE WAYS TO DESIGN WORSHIP TOGETHER

Marcia McFee

Abingdon Press
Nashville

THE WORSHIP WORKSHOP:
CREATIVE WAYS TO DESIGN WORSHIP TOGETHER

Library of Congress Cataloging-in-Publication Data

McFee, Marcia, 1962-
  The worship workshop : creative ways to design worship together / Marcia McFee.
    p. cm.
  Includes bibliographical references.
  ISBN 0-687-04634-3 (pbk. : alk. paper)
  1. Public worship. I. Title
  BV15 .M37 2002
  264—dc21

2002007273

All scripture quotations unless noted otherwise are taken from the *New Revised Standard Version of the Bible,* copyrighted 1989, Division of Christian Education of the National Council of the Churches of Christ in the United States of America. Used by permission. All rights reserved.

Scripture quotations noted NIV are taken from the HOLY BIBLE: NEW INTERNATIONAL VERSION®. Copyright © 1973, 1978, 1984 by the International Bible Society. Used by permission of Zondervan Publishing House. All rights reserved.

The poem on p. 82 by Noel Davis is from *Love Finds a Way* © 2000 and is used by permission of Shekinah Creative Centre.

The poem on p. 84 is © 1993 by Marcia McFee and was originally used in the BBC television series *Come, Holy Spirit.*

The drawing on p. 96 is by Alicia White Daily, Post Office Box 878, Forest, VA 24551. Used by permission

02 03 04 05 06 07 08 09 10 11—10 9 8 7 6 5 4 3 2 1

MANUFACTURED IN THE UNITED STATES OF AMERICA

CONTENTS

104 520

INTRODUCTION

The Worship Workshop is designed for use by a group, a gathering, a "gaggle" of people—in other words, more than one. And if one person talks and nobody talks back, that one person is still alone! The information, activities, and discussions suggested are *interactive*. I'm not merely advising this, I'm praying for it. **This, for me, is a justice issue, because liturgy belongs to *all* the people.**

The issue of "inclusive" worship pertains not just to the words we say, but also who says them, who understands them, who writes them; not just the actions we observe, but the actions we, as a *body*, participate in.

WHO PARTICIPATES IN WORSHIP?

WHO LEADS WORSHIP?

WHO PLANS WORSHIP?

WHO KNOWS ABOUT WORSHIP?

The answer to all these questions must be, "WE <u>ALL</u> DO!"

If "liturgy" literally means "work of the people," then let's put the people to work!

There are no finer reasons to call God's people together than for

- Studying the Bible
- Talking about God (doing theology)
- Studying the history of our faith practices
- Exploring, evaluating, and visioning
- Dialoguing
- Fellowshiping
- Creating

We engage in these activities when we gather to focus on worship. We learn about our history, we evaluate and celebrate our present, and we prepare for our future.

Let us enter this adventure together as the people of God!

* BEFORE YOU DO ANYTHING ELSE . . .

Wait! **Before you read another word—just breathe.**
Take a deep breath in and then sigh as you exhale.
(I'm not kidding—don't forget, this is an interactive resource!)

Worship is as necessary to our lives as breathing. This is a fairly major claim to make, and yet, as I think about what breathing does to sustain us, I can't help applying the analogies to how worship sustains us as well. Here are some observations:

> Worship is a time and place where we are *"in-spired" (to breathe in)* by the Word and the story of Jesus Christ in our midst. As God is praised, we are refreshed and replenished, given strength and new life.
>
> Worship is an opportunity to cast off, or *"ex-pire" (to breathe out)* those things which we do not need. Burdens, confessions, exhortations are given up to God. We are made new in the casting off, making room for life and love.
>
> Worship is also the experience of *"con-spiring" with (to breathe with)* the Spirit in discerning our role as the Body of Christ active in the world, bringing about the reign of God.

How can we increase the possibility that our worship will be like life-giving breath? Do we just go on hoping and praying that it will happen? Or are there also ways to *facilitate* vital and meaningful worship experiences?

A greater understanding of ourselves, our history, our creative abilities, and one other can bring about incredible excitement and facilitate deep, caring, and meaningful worship for our communities.

Moreover, it is *the community* that must be involved in this process (not just the staff or pastors). In order for "liturgy" to literally become what that word means—the work of the people—we must engage in processes to evaluate, study, and design our worship together as a community. It will be fun, inspirational, and sometimes difficult. But it is a faithful act to struggle with sometimes conflicting feelings regarding our rituals. We get to talk about what matters to us, learn about each other, and learn more about why we do the things that we do.

SO, TAKE ANOTHER BREATH . . . TOGETHER.
AND PRAY.
I AM PRAYING FOR YOU.
BLESSINGS ON YOUR JOURNEY

— *Marcia McFee*

HOW TO USE THIS RESOURCE

I want you to be your own worship consultant and I hope this resource will help you do just that! Having grown up in a small rural church in Adrian, Missouri, I know that not all churches can afford to hire a consultant to come help them take the steps necessary to enhance their worship. I have developed this book over the last ten years of doing workshops at local, regional, and national events. I wanted people to be able to take home not only the information about worship renewal, but also the interactive experiences they had during the workshop. I hope you will get the confidence you need to facilitate your own "Worship Workshop" for your worship committee, team, or even your congregation.

To help you plan, let me suggest some formats:

- ■ **An overnight retreat with staff and worship team**
- ■ **A one-day workshop for congregation or persons interested in becoming seasonal team members**
- ■ **A month-long congregational study in a combined Sunday school format**
- ■ **Regularly scheduled worship committee meetings**

Here is a sample schedule for a one-day workshop. You won't have time to get to all the material in the book in a day so this is my suggestion for a general introduction. For an overnight retreat, simply expand the number of things you do in any one of the sessions and take more time (for instance, do Session 1 on Friday night and Sessions 2, 3, and 4 on Saturday). For a month-long study, divide the sessions into four weeks. And you can pick and choose if you are simply using it as a resource for your regular worship team meeting.

8:30 - 9:00 Breakfast and Conversation

- Have newsprint on the wall with "I celebrate . . . " and "I pray . . . " (pages 22-23) and encourage people to write on them before going to their seats

9:00 Opening Worship (create your own or adapt the following)

- Create a worship center on the spot using many candles and the "Call to Worship" (pages 91-92)
- Pray using the format with "Open My Eyes, That I May See" (page 103) and substituting "A Prayer" (page 11) for the Pastoral Prayer
- Proclaim using "Metaphoraging" (page 12)

9:30 Session 1: M²: Equations for Good Worship: The Basics

- Give a short introduction to the day
- Do the "M² Worship" exercise (page 27)

- Present "The I's Have It" (pages 35-39), especially spending time reflecting on the multiple intelligences in pairs and then with the group

10:30 Break

10:45 Session 2: An Interactive Walking Tour of 3000 Years of Worship History (only the highlights!)

- Go through "How Can Tradition Help Us Change?" (pages 46-59). In order to keep it to an hour, you may want to eliminate "The Diaspora," "Out of the Closet," and "The Age of Reason"

12:00 Lunch

1:00 Session 3: The Three V's: Enhancing Our Worship

- Go over "The Three V's" (pages 40-45) as a group and then have small groups spend 15 minutes scanning and discussing the examples on pages 42-45
- Talk about dramatizing scripture by doing page 89
- Propose a hypothetical theme and let small groups imagine how they would create a worship center
- Teach the Lord's Prayer with gestures (page 100)
- Sing a global song and a song from Taizé

2:15 Break

2:30 Session 4: "If 'liturgy' literally means 'work of the people,' let's put the people to work!"

- Have a "Brainstorming Party" (page 65)
- Conclude by adding new reflections from the group to the "I celebrate . . ." and "I pray . . ." lists

3:45 Closing Worship

- Add a bowl of water to the worship center as the people gather around and sing a song (e.g., "Spirit of the Living God" or "Sanctuary")
- Thank the people and thank God for the people
- Invite everyone to touch the water and remember their baptism
- Close with a benediction

4:00 Depart

Note: To be "interactive" is to have most of the people contributing most of the time. Here are some helpful pointers to facilitate this:

■ Sit around tables of about 4-8 people. This facilitates small group discussion quickly and easily. At my workshops with worship teams from many different churches in attendance, I want churches to sit together so that they can talk specifically about their context. But in a congregational setting, you may want to occasionally mix people up so that they are not always sitting and reflecting with their family or best friends.

■ Not everyone feels comfortable talking in front of a group. Whenever possible, have people pair up or make small groups to discuss something first before bringing it to a larger group format. This helps bring out the wisdom of everyone—not just the extroverted! Allow less time for activities when partners are sharing and more time when discussion is going around the table. As a leader, you will always be interrupting conversations to move to the next activity. Don't wait for people to stop talking when they are finished—they won't. Just continually check around the room to see if most people have had the time they need.

■ Don't just talk about things—do them. For instance, if you are going to use one session with your worship team to focus on visuals, bring a bunch of stuff for the group to create several worship centers. Having had the experience, we can more readily dream of further ideas. Begin and/or end each session with a "worshipful moment" using the section on "Openers" or ideas from the chapter Utilizing Arts and Artists in the Church.

■ The exercises are designed to be done in a group setting in the moment. However, you may also want to assign certain pages to be read before your meetings in preparation for discussion.

GROUP OPENERS

A Prayer

We live in a new era and a time in which we look ahead with hopes and dreams and well-meaning resolutions! What can we pray for regarding our worship in this age? Join me in this prayer for our tasks at this time:

Creator and Sustainer God, we celebrate your presence among us at the threshold of a significant time. We know that you wrap us in your loving care and nudge us into the future. You comfort us, inspire us, and call us to contemplation and to action. Grant us the patience and the passion to do your work.

Inspire us to greater joy, God. Free us from our fears when we feel the Spirit moving within us. Let us dance, let us sing, let us shout, let us cry for the love of you. Help us to find ways to bring your Word alive.

Inspire us to greater vision. Open our eyes to the gifts and ministries of all people. Let our places of worship reflect the diverse ways that you come to us. May your Word be proclaimed through words, paint brushes, voices, bodies, and instruments. Help us to see and celebrate all that you have created.

Inspire us to compassion. As we struggle with an ever-changing world, show us the way to be with each other—even when we don't agree. Help us to know that you are there in our midst. Open our hearts wide to each other and to your possibilities for time-honored and life-giving worship.

We worship you with all that we are and all that we have. We praise you for the great things you have done! We commit to the renewal of our spirits in the awesome task of worship. We pray these things in the name of Christ, our Savior.

Amen.

"Metaphoraging"

After healing a man, Peter and John came before the rulers, elders, and teachers of the law:

> When they saw the courage of Peter and John and realized that they were unschooled, ordinary men, they were astonished and they took note that these men had been with Jesus. "What are we going to do with these men?" they asked. "Everybody living in Jerusalem knows they have done an outstanding miracle, and we cannot deny it. . . . " Then they called them in again and commanded them not to speak or teach at all in the name of Jesus. But Peter and John replied, "Judge for yourselves whether it is right in God's sight to obey you rather than God. For we cannot help speaking about what we have seen and heard."—Acts 4:13, 16, 18-20 (NIV)

A PRAYER EXPERIENCE TO GET OUR CREATIVE SELVES GOING . . .

1   Reflect on the scripture above, noticing how the author helps us see the juxtaposition between these "ordinary" men and the "outstanding" act they have done. Reflect on the ways that symbols and rituals make ordinary objects "extraordinary" (e.g., bread and water).

2   Give everyone two minutes to silently forage their pockets, their purse, or the room for an ordinary object that can represent what they hope for in this time together. Come back to encircle a table (where you have already placed a cloth, candle, and Bible), and have everyone hold on to their object until all return.

3   One at a time, have individuals place their object on the table and say a sentence prayer using the object as a metaphor. For instance:
   • *chalkboard eraser* "I pray that God will wipe away our fear."
   • *keys* "I pray that God will open the doors of our hearts to new things."
   • *plant* "I pray that we will be nourished in our faith, and flourish and grow."

4   Invite the group to respond after each one with the unison phrase, "Praise God who is in all things!"

5   When all have finished, sing a meditative refrain like "Spirit of the Living God" with a communal "Amen" at the end.

Note: This is a good exercise to get people talking about visual metaphors and utilizing "ordinary" and diverse symbols in our worship. It also brings people quickly into a deeply meaningful attitude of prayer and fellowship. We are, as I call it, "meaning mongers." Using metaphors to create meaning and symbolism is very important to our spiritual lives. Enjoy!

A Vision of "the Church"

"Do not leave Jerusalem, but wait for the gift my Father promised, which you have heard me speak about. For John baptized with water, but in a few days you will be baptized with the Holy Spirit." . . . When the day of Pentecost came, they were all together in one place. Suddenly a sound like the blowing of a violent wind came from heaven and filled the whole house where they were sitting. They saw what seemed to be tongues of fire that separated and came to rest on each of them. All of them were filled with the Holy Spirit and began to speak in other tongues as the Spirit enabled them. Acts 1:4*b*-5, 2:1-4 (NIV)

AN EXERCISE TO GET OUR CREATIVE SELVES GOING . . .

1 Divide into partners. Each pair should have a piece of blank paper and one pen or pencil.

2 Ask both partners to hold the writing utensil (yes, there will be two hands on one pen).

3 Now ask the partners to draw "the church," without giving any verbal cues to each other. Affirm that "the church" may be interpreted in many different ways.

4 After all partners have finished drawing, and before sharing the actual drawings with one another, ask the group to reflect on the experience of drawing together. What was it like? Was there a moment of revelation when both realized a common vision? How did the final vision develop? How is this experience like the mysterious movement of the Holy Spirit within the church?

5 Share your drawings with one another and reflect together on the various interpretations of the exercise.

6 As a group, offer a prayer of thanksgiving for the diverse visions of ministry and for the Spirit who makes us one. Close the prayer by singing "We are one in the Spirit, We are one in the Lord."

<u>Note:</u> Let us be reminded how important it is to begin our work, especially our work with worship, in a "worshipful" way. The exercise above demonstrates a way to get our creativity flowing by "improvising" together as well as affirming our connection to one another. Creating a brief time for "centering" the group and focusing on our sacred task will make the rest of the session more meaningful as well as productive!

"God Is Like a . . ."

"If anyone is in Christ, there is a new creation."—2 Corinthians 5:17 (NRSV)

"Using the same old materials of earth, air, fire, and water, every twenty-four hours God creates something new out of them. If you think you're seeing the same show all over again seven times a week, you're crazy. Every morning you wake up to something that in all eternity never was before and never will be again. And the you that wakes up was never the same before and will never be the same again either."—Frederick Buechner, *Wishful Thinking: A Seeker's ABC*

AN EXERCISE TO GET OUR CREATIVE SELVES GOING . . .

1 Divide into partners (three is okay, too)

2 After reading the above quotation, invite people to think of some "same old materials" of creation and write them down (these will be nouns; for example, "a door," "a tree," "a chalkboard," "a light")

3 One partner says to the other—

> "God is like a _____, because . . ."
> *(insert one of the words here)*

4 The other partner responds with how God is like that "ordinary" thing.

> For example: "God is like a door, because . . ."
> " . . . opening to God will lead to new paths."

5 Share some of these with each other in the whole group, turning it into a litany by repeating "Thanks be to God who is in all things" after each example is lifted up.

Note: It is important to "exercise" and prepare our creative selves when we gather together to work on worship just as it is important to exercise our bodies when preparing for physical work. These exercises probably won't be directly used in the final product of worship, but they are designed to help us begin to explore ideas more creatively. Buechner's quotation reminds us that creativity is available to us in an ongoing way with a Creator who surrounds us with renewal each day. The "God Is Like a . . ." exercise reminds us that Christian worship makes the "ordinary" extraordinary when we recognize how God is present with us in a diversity of ways.

HOT TOPICS

The following are some of the most important topics to consider in enhancing worship. By focusing on these topics and making small changes in each of these areas you can immediately enhance the worship experience. Under each topic discussion, two suggestions are included for your use. Remember, any changes should be undertaken with simultaneous education of the congregation. We can all worship more fully when we appreciate the biblical, theological, and historical grounding of our rituals.

Visual Metaphors

We cannot ignore that communication happens to a large extent through visual mediums. It has always been true that we glean meaning and understanding through visible symbols as well as words. But visual aids in education, information, and entertainment industries have made visual communication more commonplace; therefore we have come to expect that more of our senses will be utilized in every aspect of our lives—including our worship. So, let us expand our understanding of visuals in worship, remembering that the primary objective is always to strengthen the proclamation of the gospel, not to detract from it. Here are a couple of suggestions:

- **Create worship "environments."** Visual metaphors and symbols can be placed in a variety of places, not just on a table in the front or in the form of banners on the wall. *Example: Place a fountain of flowing water in the entrance, out of which water is gathered for a remembrance of baptism later in the service, and encourage congregants to touch the water as they leave the sanctuary as a sign of having been refreshed.* Creating environments helps us center ourselves in the message for the day immediately upon our arrival. They help us focus on the theme of the day or season. They help tell our faith story. Visuals can add depth, dimension, interest, and beauty to the worshiping space. They are images that we take away in our picture-memories (these memories often last longer than words spoken).

- **Use the "ordinary stuff" of life to create new and meaningful symbols.** *Example: Reminder notes help us create order out of our sometimes chaotic schedules. Perhaps a scripture from one of the prophets can be seen as God's way of reminding us to prioritize and take action in a chaotic world. Ask your youth group to prepare sticky notes with short scriptures of encouragement and cover the pulpit, a table, or other objects with them. As a response to the sermon, invite people to take one home to "remind" them of God's presence in their lives.* Our everyday lives are enriched and woven into our faith experience when we bring the stuff of our everyday lives into the worship experience. In this example, each time someone uses a sticky note, they will be reminded of the message that day.

Thy word is a lamp unto my feet.

Dramatic Interpretations

We are a people of an exciting story! But (I'll say it) often the story is expressed in not-so-exciting ways. Much of our worship is missing the drama of the mystery and awe inherent in our faith. People are yearning for a sense of the Spirit, perhaps something special and meaningful they experienced on a retreat or even in a movie or book. Why is it that our worship services are sometimes the last places that we experience this? Our "traditional" services often seem too "stiff"; our "contemporary" services may seem too "familiar" and are without the ritual we crave. A hot topic for worship is "ancient-future" worship. This worship draws on the ancient church's practices—delighting in the mystery of God—as well as the use of the arts (drama, visuals, and so forth) to ground us in the reality of God in our present day lives. Here are some suggestions for bringing the drama of our faith story alive in worship:

■ **Make more of already existing ritual.** Worship does not have to do away with ritual as has been tried with some "contemporary" worship. Instead ritual can help us experience the "awesome" connection to a great and mysterious God. *Example: Instead of sending acolytes down the aisle during a prelude, give the ritual of the entrance of the Light of Christ more significance by having the congregation stand and turn to watch it enter, either in silence, with a soft drumbeat, or with a meditative, repetitive congregational song like "Thy Word is a lamp unto my feet." Have one acolyte bring in the light and the other bring in the Bible or a bowl of water representing our connection through our baptism.*

■ **Dramatize scripture using several voices or interspersing passages with music.** Hearing scripture in a variety of ways helps us hear and comprehend it better, making it more memorable. The monotony of hearing it read from one place by one voice lessens its power to communicate to us. *Example: Use multigenerations of voices to emphasize the Spirit's work among all people in the scripture which proclaims, "[all readers] I will pour out my spirit on all flesh; [children] your sons and daughters will prophesy, [elders] your old ones will dream dreams, [youth] and your young ones shall see visions. [congregation] On all people, in those days I will pour out my spirit."*

Diverse Music

A good goal in this area is to use some funds to expand your church's library of song books. Give special attention to adding global music and meditative choruses and chants to your church's menu of options. Learning new songs (a little at a time) expands our vocabulary of praise and prayer. Doing so, we can affirm a multiplicity of musical yearnings in the congregation and become more aware of our connection to other Christians. As the world becomes smaller through increased opportunities for travel and information, there is a need to both stay connected to our own ethnomusical heritage and become conversant with our global neighbors through the power of song. Here are a couple of suggestions for beginning this journey:

Alleluia! Halleluja! Aleluia! HALLE! HALLE! Heleluyan! Hallelu!

- **Gather "Alleluia" songs from around the world.** Most global collections of songs will include several Alleluias. Begin a tradition of singing an Alleluia each Sunday after reciting a creed, the words of assurance, or the Gospel reading. Learn a new song for each liturgical season or month, repeating it enough for people to really learn it. Include information in the bulletin about Christians in the country from which the chorus originates.

- **Add the little book *Songs and Prayers from Taizé* to your collection of music material.** Use these short, beautiful, easy-to-learn chants as "bookends" before and after a time of prayer. This can help the congregation transition into a more meditative and attentive state and can also increase the sense of "awe" for the ritual of worship.

Liturgical Worship

"Liturgy" as it is literally meant is "the work of the people." This word has, unfortunately, taken on a diminished meaning and is sometimes even considered a "bad word" for those who are attempting to revitalize worship. However, we must reclaim it as a *key* to that very revitalization. More "liturgical" worship will use the voices and words and testimonies and artistic contributions of the people gathered. More "liturgical" worship will take seriously the idea that worship is not done *to* or *for* the people but *by* the people *for* God. Here are some suggestions for moving in this direction:

- **Use more than one "liturgist" to read the "leader" parts in a service.** Even a single litany can use many voices to read parts. Hearing a greater diversity of voices reading leader parts affirms each person's importance in the Body of Christ. This can be complemented by a single sentence response from the people repeated throughout such as, "Come thou long expected Jesus." Reading lots of words and, at the same time, comprehending them is difficult for some people. Using a simple congregational response format includes more people, making worship more intergenerational.

■ **Create seasonal worship planning teams.** Incorporating more people in the creative process provides an entry for understanding worship, faith, and spiritual growth. Incorporating the ideas of more people affirms each person's call to proclaim the presence of God in his or her life. Creating together is fun and community-building.

Liturgical Leaders as Spiritual Directors

In my view, this is the "hottest topic" for worship. My hope is that we can eliminate "plug and play" worship and begin to experience worship as a journey in which we encounter the divine and we encounter each other. Do you know what I mean by "plug and play" worship? You could also call it "fill in the blank." It is worship that's in pieces. We have an order of worship but there may not be any awareness or sense of why we progress in that order and the pieces may or may not have any relationship to each other, much less build upon each other. Let us find new meaning in our rituals and let us be open to the Spirit working actively in our midst. It is the role of liturgical leaders to facilitate both our understanding of the ritual and our participation with the Spirit in it. Here are two ways we can work toward this goal:

■ **Use a song leader to model energy.** You may or may not already have someone "leading" singing. The emphasis I want to add here is that a song leader is used to "model energy." This person is helping the congregation feel the flow and dynamics of the hymns and songs, helping them glean more meaning and heighten their experience of them. A song leader isn't someone who simply "conducts" the congregation with tempo indications, but encourages those gathered through his or her body language to join their voices together with "one accord."

Often much thought and care goes into choosing the music for each particular service. Sometimes, however, we as the congregation need to be pointed toward the reason a hymn has been selected. A song leader can do this by changing introductions from instructional remarks ("please turn to hymn number 388") to liturgical nudges like "as we turn to hymn number 388 let us prepare for prayer through Charles Wesley's words, 'O Come and Dwell in Me' (the title) and remember that the presence and the power of the Spirit frees us, according to this hymn, from our 'sorrow, fear and sin.'"

The song leader may make the decision to vary the tempo of the stanzas, according to the meaning of each one. In this particular example, the first verse of "O Come and Dwell in Me" could be done slowly, giving us time to make the petition to the Spirit to come and dwell in us. Then the stanzas could gradually build in tempo and dynamics as the hymn goes on to ask for a hastening of "the joyful day," a desire to witness, and finally to speak of "thine eternal bliss." Our experience of the hymn is radically different than if we were left to our own interpretation without the help of our song leader.

■ **Be attentive to transitions.** When I teach dance, I emphasize that the dance itself is not merely a string of steps that fit nicely together. To truly dance is to find a flow that takes the participant on a journey that leads easily and interestingly from one point to another. This flow is created by giving attention to how we transition from one thing to the next. Our Christian ritual is a dance and a journey. The fourfold order of *gathering, proclaiming, responding*, and *sending forward* (you can work creatively within this order) is an ancient order that embodies (dances) our faith. To relegate the pieces to a list to be checked off one at a time robs us of the beauty and flow of good ritual (worship). Transitions are not just a time of "announcing" the next thing. They are, in and of themselves, opportunities for proclamation, prayer, and teaching. For example, rather than saying, "Let us now greet one another," turn the moment into a time for inspiration:

"Jesus said that wherever two or three [or more] are gathered, there he would be also. 'Emmanuel'—God with us. And so, I invite you to greet the Christ in each other by saying 'Shalom to you, friend.'" (The greeting time might end with the choir leading "Shalom to You," continuing the theme as well as providing a fluid transition into the next portion of the service.)

These kinds of transitions are not something that everyone feels comfortable doing off the top of their head. I write out nearly all of my transitions. I don't *read* them, but at least I have given each one clear and prayerful consideration beforehand. And then when the Spirit presents a different direction, I am ready and willing to recognize it and acknowledge it because I have prepared and can follow the Spirit in worship.

Musical refrains, instrumental or vocal, can also help us transition. An instrument such as a flute or violin can litter the service with a musical theme that the congregation then discovers in the last hymn. Be aware that not every transition requires words from a leader or music or even an announcement as to what is next. Sometimes you can simply let the bulletin do its job as a worship guide and an indicator of what is coming up. As you begin to see the service as a journey with varying dynamics, you will be able to discern when it is appropriate and helpful to provide transitions and when it is better to go right from a hymn, for example, into a prayer.

Another helpful ingredient to transitions, mood, and energy is lighting levels and visuals. If you have subtle control over lighting in the sanctuary (dimmer switches for overhead lights), you can lower the lighting during introspective times, such as prayer. If you have the capability for visual projections, consider adding images relating to the theme of the upcoming song or litany. For example, you could project photos of light through windows as you sing a preparatory song and pray a Prayer of Illumination before the sermon.

REFLECTION

After reading the section on Hot Topics, spend some time reflecting together on what perhaps sparked your interest, made you excited, left you puzzled, or simply made you say "Yes!" or "Hmmm. . . ." If you need help getting the conversation started, split up into pairs or smaller groups to discuss the following questions; then reconvene as a group to jump-start the group's discussion with your reflections. This could also be used as a worship team "homework assignment" in preparation for a meeting.

What are the "hot topics" for our church at present?

Do we use visuals creatively? Do they help us tell the Story?

How diverse are our music selections? Do we use music in other ways besides preludes, hymns, and anthems?

Do we have a healthy mix of order and mystery?

Is scripture read in the same manner every Sunday?

Do we have a model of energy in our service? What are the energy dynamics? Do they vary?

CHAPTER 1

CHANGE? FIRST, LET'S

Evaluate!

Don't get tense at the mention of the word "evaluate." Inside that word is the root word "value." It is important to talk about what we value about our worship. In doing so, we remember the significance of the words and actions that give expression to our worship, and we begin to speak openly about our relationship to our God, whom we worship. It can be a wonderful way to deepen our relationship with each other as well.

There are many ways to evaluate our present worship. The following pages suggest several exercises that can guide your evaluation. However, the one ingredient that is necessary in all cases is a *loving and caring environment* where each person has a voice *without fear of judgment*. This environment cannot be assumed; it must be verbalized at the beginning of the group's time together. Start with prayer and an overt statement that everyone is invited to learn and dialogue together.

And remember, breathe.

In addition, remember to use language of affirmation and hope. This does not mean we should shy away from challenge, but a group that sees challenge as opportunity rather than obstacle will be able to go deeper in its discussions.

The next two pages, "I celebrate that worship at my church is . . . " and "I pray that worship at my church will be . . . " are worksheets that I often hand to people at the beginning of a workshop. I ask them to take a moment to list things they celebrate about their worship already (affirming what we are already doing), and what they pray for worship to be (using positive language to talk about what we yearn for). This is a good way for worship teams to get feedback from the congregation or simply get the conversation started about where they are concerning worship.

Here is another exercise. Place a large piece of paper on a wall or table where people enter with the title:

"OUR CHURCH IS . . . "

Invite people to use markers to write "graffiti style" words that complete the sentence, such as "friendly," "warm," "fun," "jazzed about mission," "beautiful." Later in the session substitute the word "worship" for "church" so that it reads, **"Our worship is. . . . "** Now look at the same words and discern if there is a discrepancy between how we identify ourselves and how we worship as a community.

EXERCISE!

I CELEBRATE THAT WORSHIP AT MY CHURCH IS . . .

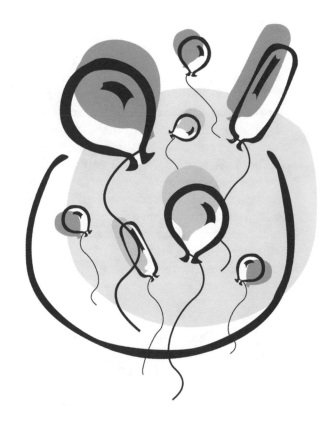

From *The Worship Workshop: Creative Ways to Design Worship Together,* by Marcia McFee. Copyright 2002 by Abingdon Press. Reproduced by permission.

I PRAY THAT WORSHIP AT MY CHURCH WILL BE . . .

WORSHIP HAS BEEN FOR ME . . .

Evaluating and Celebrating Our Worship

There are so many important questions to consider when evaluating and celebrating worship. Asking questions and discussing dreams and disappointments in a caring context is imperative in order to develop a clear, strong vision for the role of worship in our spiritual growth. In addition to focusing on whether worship holds our attention, whether it is interesting and inspirational, and whether it "meets our needs," we are called to reflect *theologically* on the scope and span of that which we proclaim in worship. Do we proclaim that which is "comfortable" to us? Do we choose content based on what we think people want to hear or experience? Do we have a healthy balance of comfort and challenge in worship?

The following group activity is designed to help us look at this question:
"Are we proclaiming the fullness of the gospel to which we are called?"

1   Make copies of the "Worship has been for me . . . " page for distribution to each person gathered.
2   Make sure everyone recalls the stories listed. If needed, read the story or have the group tell it in their own words.
3   With the whole group, brainstorm a list of descriptive/feeling words for each story. Each person should write all words offered on their paper. For example, "The Wedding Feast"' may have words such as "celebration," "invitation," "transformation." Whereas, "The Garden of Gethsemane" may include "agony," "earnest prayer," "meditative."
4   Divide into partners and together reflect on:
    your own personal experience of worship (for example, "'The Sermon on the Mount' was emphasized in the church where I grew up because of a focus on preaching.")
    your own worship preference (for example, "I wish worship was more celebratory like 'The Wedding Feast.'")
    where your congregation fits in (for example, "We do 'The Sermon on the Mount' and 'The Road to Emmaus' [encounter with Christ] very well, but we don't model community and forgiveness like 'The Last Supper.'")
5   As a whole group once again, take a poll to compare answers. Discuss whether or not the fullness of the gospel story is reflected in your worship and why that may be the case. For example, is worship a place where we know we can celebrate and also mourn? be on a journey together? experience the abundance of God? be outraged at the injustices of the world? Are we afraid to laugh, cry, touch, sing, or proclaim? Why? Of course, all of these dynamics will not be evident in each service. It is important to remember that observing the seasons of the liturgical year can help us find opportunities to express the fullness of the gospel story.

WORSHIP HAS BEEN FOR ME . . .

The Wedding Feast

The Fishes and the Loaves

The Sermon on the Mount

JESUS OVERTURNS THE TABLES

The Last Supper

The Garden of Gethsemane

The Road to Emmaus

M²: EQUATIONS FOR GOOD WORSHIP

We are *all* experts at worship! Simply by virtue of our experience of worshiping, we know how to recognize and design good worship. It's just that we don't always have the language to consciously talk about it. And we probably haven't spent much time analyzing our experiences. This exercise encourages us to engage in the act of remembering worship experiences that were:

> "Meaningful"
> x
> "Memorable"

There is so much that goes into designing good worship, but we can discover what we already know by recalling and analyzing worship experiences whose equations were "M²." You know what kind of services I'm talking about! They are services that you can still recall and in doing so you get goose bumps because the experience touched you in a deep way.

So, in partners or small groups (or if it is a small group to begin with, you might choose to do this together), briefly describe a service that stuck with you—that was meaningful and memorable. Write these under the "Yes! Here is an example" section on the next page. Then describe what happened. What images, words, or actions do you remember *specifically*? Write these things under the "What about the experience made it . . ." section. Do this with as many services as you have time or memory for!

Now it is time to *analyze* and *reflect*. We can glean larger concepts and characteristics from specific examples and details.

MANY PEOPLE USE THE EXAMPLE OF A "CHRISTMAS EVE CANDLELIGHT COMMUNION SERVICE"

They list these types of memories about it:
- the church was decorated beautifully
- the story of the birth was acted out
- children were involved in the service
- taking communion in candlelight was awesome

Now, what characteristics could we name from this example?
- we are hungry for visuals that create a worshipful environment
- dramatizing the story helps us experience its power and meaning
- intergenerational worship feels more like everyone is involved
- we are hungry for some mystery and awe in our worship

All of these things, then, can help us create more meaningful and memorable worship in the future. It's not that we recreate old services, but we keep the equation of good worship in mind as we design.

HAVE YOU EVER EXPERIENCED "M²" WORSHIP?

Yes! Here is an example:

WHAT ABOUT THAT EXPERIENCE MADE IT *"meaningful" and "memorable"*? (BE SPECIFIC.)

WHAT CAN WE SAY ARE CHARACTERISTICS OF
GOOD WORSHIP AS A RESULT OF THESE MEMORIES?

DIAGNOSIS: WORSHIP

A Checkup for the Body of Christ

Have you ever left a worship team meeting exhausted? feeling like you got nowhere? wondering if anything will ever happen to get certain people to cross "party lines"? Whether people are of differing generations or theological backgrounds, there are always disagreements about how to worship. If this feels like your church, the following exercise, "Diagnosis: Worship," may help your worship team get to the bottom of the matters that keep them stagnant. This metaphorical device is one that I have found helpful.

Many of us don't talk very much in our worship teams about the "health" of our worship practices, our understanding of those practices, and our relationship to each other. But any conflict can be seen as creating "dis-ease" among us. Instead of staying focused on the symptoms, do a thorough checkup to see what kind of remedy can be proposed (and don't forget, there is always more than one way to treat a disease). For additional help, a wonderful resource on the subject is *Trouble at the Table: Gathering the Tribes for Worship* by Tom Troeger and Carol Doran. Read the following descriptions and make responses about your own church's worship on the handout (page 30).

1 **Patient history:** A doctor would never prescribe or diagnose without knowing something of the patient's medical history. Often our worship conflicts have roots in unresolved grief or old, unfinished issues. For example, we are a church with older charter members which has an influx of new members moving into a growing neighborhood.

2 **Symptoms** and the **dis-ease** these symptoms point to: Simply trying to "fix" a symptom without diagnosing the underlying problem is like putting a bandage on an infected wound. There may be an unspoken or even unconscious fear or misunderstanding behind a symptom. For example, the "symptom" of dis-ease could be a squabble over using different kinds of candles other than the brass candlesticks given "in memory of" Aunt Betty at the time of the start of the church. This squabble is not just about someone acting "inflexible." The disease itself is probably an underlying (and justified) fear that the past is being forgotten, that memories of the church and the contributions of its founding members are slipping away. Additionally, we have forgotten that the symbol (the light) is ultimately to remind us of Christ, not just Aunt Betty or not just to use "cool stuff." This points to problems with the understanding of symbolism. The theology of "stuff" (as I call it) is lacking depth.

3 Emergency procedures: Recognizing what the symptoms point to is the first step to resolving the conflict. What else must be done immediately in order to begin to heal? In our example, the worship team could prepare a service of remembrance and celebration where the stories of the beginnings of the church are handed down to the new "generation" (including how Aunt Betty herself was the light of Christ to many people). All Saints Sunday is a great time for this. Make a tradition of getting out *all* of the memorial gifts as well as pictures and stories for display that day. Putting Aunt Betty's candlesticks in the closet for a while will then be less traumatic and you can begin to use a diversity of materials for the symbol of the light of Christ in our midst. Additionally, education about why we use candles and the theological grounding for it will help us as a congregation to grow in our ability to worship God.

4 Preventive medicine: Once we have come to an understanding about the root of the problem, what can we do to make sure the symptoms don't reoccur? For example, use a great variety of worship settings on the table for different seasons so that we don't have an "either/or" situation.

5 Nutritional information/balanced diet: Our tendency in change is to overdo it. Change happens slowly and the balance of old and new is needed in the first stages of a new way of doing things. For example, don't wait an entire year to bring the brass candlesticks back out for a Sunday or season.

6 Sense of well-being: The beauty of dealing with "dis-eases" in a healthy way is that we open the conversation to look at other aspects of our worship. How healthy and balanced are we in other areas? Can we use our successes to raise other issues (lovingly)? For example, perhaps talking about why we had conflict about the candles will help us talk about reasons why we experience tension with regard to certain music, texts, and actions (is the dis-ease nostalgia, unfamiliarity, fear?).

DIAGNOSIS: WORSHIP

PATIENT HISTORY:

SYMPTOMS: DIS-EASE:

EMERGENCY PROCEDURES:

PREVENTIVE MEDICINE:

NUTRITIONAL INFORMATION/BALANCED DIET:

SENSE OF WELL-BEING:

THE POLITICS OF CHANGE

Change isn't easy (I bet you've never heard that before!). Any type of change must be accompanied with a great deal of love and care for one another. The most frequently asked question in my workshops is, *"How do you go about making change without upsetting people?"*

Well, of course, you can't control how everyone will react. But you can go about revitalizing worship in a more grassroots way that will make everyone feel more included and informed. Here are the four major things that I have found helpful in going about change.

TALK ABOUT IT, TALK ABOUT IT, TALK ABOUT IT!

Worship is the "work of the people," and as such should matter to people. We must be in the habit of talking about what matters to us—what is meaningful to us. I highly recommend that you don't try to "sneak" change into your worship. I believe we can give people more credit for flexibility given the chance to learn and talk about worship. When a level of trust is achieved, temporary change can be introduced without as much preparation as may be needed early in the process.

TAKE INCREMENTAL STEPS!

Don't try to pack in too many changes at once. There will be different degrees of readiness for change. Pay attention to growth of the "Body." Continue to emphasize the need to offer a diversity of ways to praise the Divine who is known in endless ways. Offer occasional special opportunities for alternative worship for those who are impatient for new things.

EDUCATION! EDUCATION! EDUCATION!

I can't stress this enough. I have seen such positive differences in congregations who study the history and theology of worship together. Always accompany changes with information about the theological, biblical, and historical significance of the new symbol or act.

PARTICIPATION!

Get more people involved in worship design and leadership. I believe that the team model of worship planning (pages 60-61) will help a lot by giving people a chance to learn and give input to worship. In a way, they take more ownership of what happens on Sunday morning. When we give of ourselves, we gain more from our participation.

SUGGESTIONS FOR STARTING A NEW SERVICE

Often churches jump to the conclusion that in order to settle worship "controversy," the solution of two services of different styles should be adopted. While this can be helpful, it is only one solution to the need for diversity and can sometimes simply mask the real underlying problem: a lack of commitment to understand one another deeply. Embark on a congregational study of worship using this book in order to dialogue in a more "healthy" atmosphere about what steps are needed. Then consider these options:

If outgrowing the sanctuary isn't the problem, diversifying the existing worship service may be possible with added trust and understanding. Also, adding special services with a diversity of expression during appropriate times in the liturgical year may be a way to enhance your church's worship life (e.g., weekly Taizé services during Lent or "praise" services from Easter to Pentecost).

By all means, consider starting another service! This can literally be a "growing" experience. What a blessing to have several opportunities for people to express their love of God. My advice is to consider it a mission endeavor. Get the support of the congregation in the way you might for a new church plant—prayers, money, and enthusiasm.

GATHER INFORMATION

- Who is the target group? What needs are there? What time slot is most conducive?
- Visit other churches to observe the possibilities.
- Read resources on starting and sustaining new services.

HONE SKILLS

- Find music and worship planning mentors in other churches and plan a training day with your leadership group.
- Begin to expand your library of worship resources.

IDENTIFY PLANNING PERSONNEL/WORSHIP TEAM MEMBERS

- Gather a worship team comprising staff, established members, and target group members.
- Have an initial brainstorming session about needs, resources, and goals (What additions to current leadership will be needed? Are modifications to the space needed? Additional equipment? What is our time line?).

PLAN A SERIES OF SERVICES

- Use the time line for Seasonal Planning Teams on page 62.
- Plan for a time period of six weeks or a season, giving yourself permission to evaluate after that time period. Plan another series, incorporating changes if necessary (e.g., a different time slot, space, or format). This allows you to have trial periods rather than starting something you have to painfully end if you don't get the response you hoped for.

SUPPORT THE ENDEAVOR

- To avoid an "us" and "them" attitude, pray in each service that the participants of the other service will be fed spiritually and that God will be praised wholeheartedly!
- Get commitments from many people to attend both the new service and their regular service for a time so that both services will have good energy and a chance to make the adjustment. What an offering of love!

CHAPTER 2

DIVERSE *Designs* FOR CONGREGATIONAL WORSHIP

As we begin to explore what it means to create and design together, it is important to discuss basic beliefs about worship. It is also important to have the community of worshipers in mind as we carry on our discussions. So, first let me suggest that you do a "Who, what, whose?" exercise for that purpose. Make a chart on the wall that looks something like the following and list answers below each heading:

Who are we?	*What matters to us?*	*Whose are we?*
For example, we are young, we are older, we are commuters, we are farmers, we are diverse kinds of families, and so forth. From what different perspectives will we experience the Story?	*For example, we worry about money, we are rushed, we are alone, we are in pain, we have a specific situation in our community at the moment, and so forth. How will these things affect our experience of worship? Will we find something that speaks to our situation?*	*How will the previous questions interact with the fact that we are the people of God, that there is good news to proclaim?*

This is about setting context. These three things *must* be kept in mind at all times when we design worship. The last one is imperative. Talk show hosts, inspirational authors, and motivational speakers do "Who are we?" and "What matters to us?" very well. But Christian worship says that the answer to "*Whose* are we?" makes a difference in the way that we deal with the first two. It is because of the good news of Christ among us that we are able to praise, pray, and be strengthened in our daily lives.

I encourage you to keep this chart in a visible place as you continue your study and creative work. Check out the things you create and write from different people's perspectives (for example, nontraditional families, persons who have just experienced loss, and so forth). When we acknowledge the real lives and difficulties of the people, we will more likely provide a meaningful environment for the Spirit to work among us.

Before we begin looking at some basic ingredients for worship (the "I's" and the "V's"), let's recognize two very strong human desires that we share with the Creator:

THE NEED FOR *Ritual*

- God's creation is full of cycles
- We all crave and create some repetition in our lives

THE NEED TO *Engage*

- God came to us incarnated in the person of Jesus
- We also have the need to belong, to interact with each other

We need a *blending* of these two things. Often, we have made the mistake of emphasizing ritual at the expense of warmth in our "traditional" worship. And in our alternative styles we have emphatically embraced interaction and personal warmth to such a degree that we often feel hungry for some sense of ritual that speaks of the awesomeness of our God.

Blending isn't just about style or music; it is about blending our understanding of what it means to worship, blending our community in a way that honors our diversity and ultimately provides a way to care for diverse needs. It involves imagination and integration.

Imagination and *integration* are the two most important skills in worship design. We must nurture our imagination so that the Story is told in exciting and diverse ways. We must also work to integrate the parts of the liturgy with diverse forms of expression. We can no longer have "plug and play" worship, which keeps the parts separate and designs by filling in the blanks. The worship service must be seen holistically—certainly with structure and form, but one that serves to take us on a journey of *gathering, proclaiming, responding,* and *sending forth.*

> *imagination* = **the act of creating images**
>
> *integration* = **the act of connecting the parts with INTEGRITY**

Whoa! There is *that* word! How many times has "integrity" been spoken with fear and trepidation by those who want to compare one style with another? Let us reclaim the power of this word as true for *all* forms of worship. We must have worship with integrity no matter the style we use. Certainly theological integrity for the words we speak, the songs we sing, and the images we use is necessary! We should always be evaluating this. But there are many other things that go into worship that has "integrity."

THE I'S HAVE IT

In designing worship that has integrity, think of the four "I's": interactive, intergenerational, interesting, and inspirational.

Interactive Worship

Interactive worship is participatory worship. This is the way I describe it:

IN PARTICIPATORY WORSHIP, SOMETHING HAPPENS!

We believe that the Spirit enables transformation. But do we really expect that this will happen? Do we expect to feel a connection to the divine? To open ourselves up to the possibility that we will be somehow different when we leave than when we came is to participate with the Spirit in the renewal of the Body of Christ.

PARTICIPATORY WORSHIP IS "ENGAGING"!

One of my favorite TV characters is Captain Jean-Luc Picard of the Starship *Enterprise*. He gives the coordinates to the pilot and then looks straight ahead, points his finger forward, and commands, "Engage!" The starship blasts off with a mighty whoosh, and the stars whiz by in an exciting rush of energy. Is this what happens for us at the end of worship? Have we engaged with the Word of God to such an extent that we are sent with vital energy into the world to do the work of God? Or do we putter along, acting more like a Model T? Does worship engage our senses, our intellect, and our spirit?

PARTICIPATORY WORSHIP ELICITS A RESPONSE

Responses come in many forms. It could be that we have been inspired to some kind of action. Perhaps we respond with new convictions and beliefs that we carry with us. It may be that we are drawn to respond and reflect around the dinner table with others. No matter the form of the response, participatory worship lives beyond the time and place of the ritual. It goes with us, and we are moved to do something as a result.

PARTICIPATORY WORSHIP PERMEATES THE "FOURTH WALL"

This expression comes from my background in the theater. When we talk of a performer who permeates the "fourth wall" (the imaginary wall between stage and audience), we are saying that a performer has such energy that they seem to reach right out to the audience and make people feel as if they are involved in the action. Participatory worship permeates the imaginary boundary between the chancel area and the congregation. Action and energy and worship take place in the whole of the sanctuary, not just "up front." Worship is something that the people *do,* not what is *done to or for them.*

PARTICIPATORY WORSHIP IS INCLUSIVE!

This is more than simply the kind of language we use for the Divine. I want us to broaden our conversation about inclusion to talk about what style of language we use (is it different from our "everyday" language? is it accessible to all ages? is it the "voice of the people"?). Also, who designs and leads worship? Does it include staff *and* laity? Is our space accessible to all who desire to participate?

> "When the preacher and the singers do everything, and there is no active engagement on the part of the remaining congregation, hope remains at best only talked or sung about."
>
> —Don Saliers, *Worship Come to Its Senses*

Intergenerational Worship...

IS INTERACTIVE.

• allows people to *be with* one another, learn from one another, worship *together;* uses many different foci in the room

USES MANY DIFFERENT WAYS TO COMMUNICATE.

• acknowledges that we *all* learn and communicate differently and that we live in a world that uses all the senses

USES MANY DIFFERENT PEOPLE TO COMMUNICATE.

• proclamation is shared by all ages; remember to use children, youth *and* seniors to lead liturgy or read scripture—and not just on "special Sundays" like youth Sunday

DOESN'T ASSUME THE ABILITY TO READ EASILY.

• some haven't learned to read and some have diminished eyesight; provide large print bulletins and use one-phrase repetitive responses for liturgies like "This is the day that the Lord has made!", "Praise God in the sanctuary!", and others that don't require lots of reading in order to participate

DOESN'T ASSUME THE ABILITY TO HEAR EASILY.

• make sure printed words are available to those who would benefit from them; provide a "worship script" that includes all words that aren't going to be in the bulletin; buy multiple cordless microphones so that many voices can be amplified at once

DOESN'T ASSUME THE ABILITY TO MOVE EASILY.

• language affirms a diversity of participation, including observation: *"I invite you to stand if you are comfortable standing, and if sitting is what you do best, I invite you to sit with gusto"*; again, the best money you can spend is for cordless microphones so that people with limited mobility can read from their place in the congregation

USES INCLUSIVE LITURGICAL LANGUAGE.

• uses resources geared to various age groups in their own language; using the term "men" to mean all people not only excludes women, but also *children;* using diverse imagery to describe God validates our *wide* range of experiences of the divine!

Interesting Worship

"Of course worship should be interesting," you say. "After all, we would like for people to be interested in praising God and telling the good news!"

WELL? *Is it interesting?*

Worship should be and can be interesting and creative. What does "creative" mean? The dictionary says it refers to something "new." However, when I use the words "creative" and "worship" together, I mean *"diverse"* worship. We do not have to "throw the baby out with the bath water" in order to revitalize worship. We come from a rich tradition—one characterized by diversity, as you will see in the history tour in chapter 3. We must draw from our past and the rituals our predecessors "handed down" and "surrendered" to us (the literal meanings of the Latin for tradition), as well as find meaningful ways to tell the Story in *our* time and place.

Why do we need diverse worship? Because we learn and communicate in diverse ways. An educational theory by Howard Gardner says that we relate to things in ways that make "sense" to us, in the ways we are adept. It is called *multiple intelligences theory,* and it states that we each fall into different categories of "intelligences." Even though Gardner didn't relate this theory to the worship experience, I can imagine how it could work. Following are the seven intelligences and how they can relate to worship:

LINGUISTIC INTELLIGENCE

Those who are strong is this category glean meaning from words. The sermon may be the highlight, the most instructive moment in the service for them. Our society has put a higher value on this kind of intelligence, but we do not all fall into this category.

MUSICAL INTELLIGENCE

This category includes people who come to church for the music. They hear the message and are inspired through the music. It doesn't necessarily mean they have extraordinary musical talent, but they have a high appreciation for it.

LOGICAL–MATHEMATICAL INTELLIGENCE

When there is a theme that is evident and grows in the service from beginning to end, logical-mathematical people are greatly satisfied. They like a logical progression of ideas and can notice even the subtle references and similarities between the parts of the service.

SPATIAL INTELLIGENCE

Environment is very important to spatial people. They notice their surroundings and glean meaning from visuals, worship centers, and diverse placement of readers and musicians. An environment that never changes is monotonous to them.

BODILY-KINESTHETIC INTELLIGENCE

Actions are important in this intelligence. These people might prefer to have communion every Sunday. The "act" of embodying the Word is valuable, and dramatic interpretations are also very satisfying for them.

INTRAPERSONAL INTELLIGENCE

Mystery, awe, silence, and meditative reflection are what feel "holy" and "reverent" to these strongly intrapersonal folk. If they don't have a chance for reflection in the service, it may not feel like they have "worshiped."

INTERPERSONAL INTELLIGENCE

Fellowship with others is highly important for those in this category. They like the time for passing the peace and the opportunities for sharing in small groups. A more "communal" and warm style of worship is their preference.

What categories do we find ourselves in? Discuss together and then talk about what may be true for other members of the congregation. Which intelligences does our worship most cater to? Which intelligences don't get to experience their particular communication style?

Here is the incredible value I have witnessed in seeing groups study this theory. We become aware that there is a reason for our differences. We become aware that:

It isn't a generational thing. Often we make the mistake of thinking that the "younger" generation wants more music and the "older" generation wants more words. In reality, these preferences exist in every generation!

It isn't a personal thing. We aren't "out to get each other."

It doesn't need to be a divisive thing.

For example, people who prefer intrapersonal communication and learning may complain about energetic singing (and clapping). But becoming aware of their particular "intelligence" preference and the fact that others (especially bodily-kinesthetic people) need different kinds of communication styles can help them "tolerate" those parts of the service that do not appeal directly to them. This knowledge may even release them to enjoy this gift for others *because they then trust that their preferences will also be recognized and valued*. We may even be able to become a more caring Christian community, concerned that *all* in the Body are being strengthened in their faith.

Inspirational Worship

TO "INSPIRE" IS LITERALLY TO "BREATHE IN"

Does the good news fill us in our worship? Do we take it into our very bodies and carry it into the world? Does it "stick with us" beyond the time and place of worship? Does it replenish us like good air provides oxygen for our cells?

We have already paid attention to this matter in the exercise identifying "who we are" (our identities), "what matters to us" (our context), and "whose we are" (the difference that being a Christian makes in our identity and context). All three of these are absolutely necessary for inspirational worship. We must proclaim "whose we are" and what difference that makes in our lives for worship to be both relevant *and* inspirational.

"To be *boring* is to *bear false witness*,"

says Tom Driver in *Liberating Rites: Understanding the Transformative Power of Ritual*, another book I highly recommend for your study. Take a moment and reflect upon what he is saying. Write your comments below:

_____

_____

_____

_____

_____

_____

_____

_____

"Bear false witness . . . " to what? We are the people of an exciting story! But let's dispel a popular notion. Many who want to change and revitalize worship use the term "boring" to mean "traditional"! However, I have seen boring in *every* style of worship. Our job then is to create life-giving, inspirational worship in *any* style of worship. So no matter whether you use a more formal or informal or blended or jazzy or contemplative style, the question is the same: Is it inspirational?

THE THREE V'S

Every teacher has a way of organizing the important questions. Well, this is mine. When looking at worship, I always analyze the diversity and inclusiveness of the services I'm working on by asking the following questions that deal with three "V's":

Verbal

Whose voices do we hear? How many?

Is there a balance of lay and clergy?

Where do the voices come from?

What kind of verbal portraits do we paint of the Divine?

Whose perspectives do we hear?

What does our worship sound like?

Visual

What about the drama and aesthetic of worship?

How does the environment contribute to the focus of the service?

Where does the action take place?

Do textures and colors and art forms lend to the message of the worship?

Visceral

How is Christ's purpose lived out in our actions?

Do we as a community model the reign of God in our worship?

How do we allow a response which "embodies" the focus?

How is *what* we do integral to the message?

How do we interact with the verbal and the visual?

Specific "Three V" Questions for Designing Worship:

VERBAL

■ What songs do we know or can we find that help us sing about the theme?

■ What sounds (instrumental) would be especially meaningful to the service?

■ What scriptures would be easy to dramatize using many voices, unusual placement of readers, or interspersed music?

■ What prayers and litanies could we write or find that would use creative and diverse metaphors for God?

VISUAL

■ What could a worship center look like for this service?

■ What kind of "visual metaphors" (objects or props) could help?

■ How could a visual metaphor live beyond the service as a reminder (for example, something to take home)?

VISCERAL

■ What kind of set-up of the room would help symbolize the message?

■ What can we do to respond to the message? Could we take communion? break into small prayer circles? interact with the worship center? be commissioned to a special mission focus?

"THREE V" EXAMPLES: VERBAL

■ Use readers and liturgists who would add some significance to a theme. For example, "weaving"—quilters' group; "comfort"—health care workers; "God's creation"—gardeners.

■ Position readers in unusual places: in the back or balcony, in the middle of the center aisle, scattered in the congregation, in the choir, surrounding the congregation.

■ Have Sunday school classes or even administrative committees write liturgies based on upcoming themes. Invite them to write several statements like "Hope is. . . ." These statements can be fashioned into a call and response litany.

■ Use diverse sounds, even prerecorded "nature" sounds to accompany a psalm about God's creation. Use diverse instrumentation, including percussion instruments such as drums, rainsticks, and rattles. Place instrumentalists around the periphery of the congregation for a "surround sound" effect. This works especially well with bells or chimes. Combine sounds and words for a more interesting effect.

■ Use secular songs (like "Lean on Me" or "I'll Be There") that are appropriate to the theme as calls to prayer, responses to the Word, or introits. Use familiar tunes with new words to ease into using new music. Put a different rhythm to an old standard. For example, try singing "Jesus Loves Me" in a jazz style.

■ Use poetry and prose. Combine "ancient sayings" (scripture) with "contemporary sayings" (more recent authors and poets). Preachers often use this in a sermon, but we rarely consider poetry as fodder for liturgy. This is also an excellent way to introduce perspectives from other cultures.

■ Use music as part of the liturgy, rather than just as hymns, anthems, and "special music." For examples, see the Music section on pages 102-105.

■ Use drama in several different ways. Use short skits to introduce themes. Dramatize scripture simply by using different voices for narrative parts (even the congregation) or using several different readers. See more about this in the Dramatizing section on pages 90-92.

■ Practice more silence! Take time to prepare for silence with a sung refrain or chiming bell, and ease out of silence in a similar way. Give the congregation specific things to meditate on or pray about during the silence. We don't know how to embrace silence in our hectic time, but we crave it. Focus on it as a spiritual discipline.

"THREE V" EXAMPLES: VISUAL

■ Go beyond banners! Begin to think of visuals as not only two-dimensional objects, but as worship "environments" that teach, draw us into the service, create anticipation, and help us with the task of praying or worshiping.

■ Use "worship centers." These are crafted presentations of objects, colors, and symbols that point us in the direction of the Story or theme. Use pottery, for example, when worshiping God as the "potter." For more examples of this, see the Visuals section on pages 93-94

■ Consider alternatives to front and center as the placement for worship centers. Create smaller "off-center centers" in the aisles, at the back, or in the nave so that people can encounter them at a closer distance when they arrive or interact with them during the service. For instance, for a baptismal remembrance service, create a worship center in the front using the font but also have pitchers of water and bowls in the aisles around the congregation. Have several people pour water for another experience of "surround sound."

■ Think asymmetrical. No rule says that a table must be set with two candlesticks on either side of the cross with a Bible directly in front of it. One candle to the side (or two) or three candles of different heights in a triangular pattern is absolutely appropriate. There is theological significance for each of these. Also, use different kinds of candleholders and candles. Many people have beautiful ones in their homes, which can be borrowed for a Sunday or season, and they would probably be thrilled!

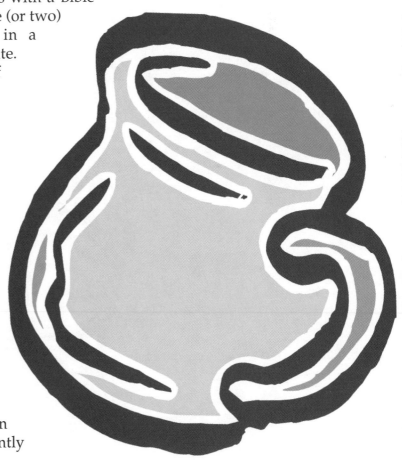

■ Be creative with colors. Don't always use primary colors. There are many ways to represent the liturgical season in the sanctuary. It may be more appropriate on a Sunday in Lent, for example, to use coarse burlap (sackcloth). "Shiny" fabric is not always the most appropriate either. Instead, consider using other cloth items, such as quilts, if there is a focus on who we are—all pieces woven together as one. Commission someone who goes to a fabric store frequently to be on the lookout for discount fabrics.

■ Sometimes dried arrangements of greenery are more appropriate than fresh flowers—perhaps when telling the story of baby Moses hidden in the reeds. Work with those in charge of flowers "given in honor of" in order to avoid difficult situations. A separate flower stand other than on the worship center is one way to alleviate conflicts.

■ Use diverse bulletin covers rather than pictures of the church on the cover! There are many wonderful computer clip art images and graphics. Use images that help tell the Story. Use artwork created by children, youth, or artists in the congregation.

■ Use diverse lighting if you have it. Make sure that lights focus on worship centers, rather than just the pulpit. If you have dimmers, dim the lights during prayer to set the environment for introspection.

■ Use PowerPoint or other computer software, slides, or video projections if available to create yet another kind of visual worship center. For example, while worshiping using the text of Jesus calling the disciples to be "fishers of people" at the seashore, use images on a screen of lakes, water, beaches, fishing boats. These images help transport us to the scene and engage our imagination.

■ Use PowerPoint software, slides, or video to project announcements as people are entering and leaving the sanctuary. This could solve the everlasting question, *Where do we place the announcements in the service so they won't be "disruptive"?*

"THREE V" EXAMPLES: VISCERAL

■ Always ask yourselves, *What can we do that will "embody" the Word proclaimed?* In other words, *How can we "practice what we preach"?* Visceral experiences ("viscera" means "gut") trigger something that connects with our experience of life. We are "touched" in a deep way because we know it in our gut.

■ Use different places in the sanctuary for different readings. For example, if you are reading from the Psalms, "get you up to a high mountain," have the reader read from the balcony with a loud voice, creating the feeling that he or she is calling to the congregation. Or if the words say, "comfort my people," have the reader read from the aisle, lightly touching the shoulders of a few people in a comforting gesture. This will help us to experience the scripture in a deeper way.

■ Think of dramatic devices (not necessarily "drama") that will express a part of the liturgy in a meaningful way. For example, during a prayer for God to be with us "as a parent who reassures a child," have a parent and child sit in a rocking chair in the chancel area. They could either read the prayer or simply act as a visual metaphor.

■ Use congregational movement to underscore the purpose of a part of the liturgy. Congregational movement doesn't have to mean *dance*. It could be as simple as turning to face each other across the center aisle while saying a creed (since it is a part of the liturgy where we say who we are as Christians, let us say it to each other).

■ Target the sense of smell. The smell of baking bread from the kitchen could make communion a special event. Using various kinds of loaves could add significance on World Communion Sunday.

■ Include a sense of touch. Visual worship centers can be even more enhanced by tangible symbols that can be taken home. For instance, if you are focusing on the metaphor of God as our "rock and our redeemer," using a worship center with large rocks and having small rocks for each person to hold provides a direct connection to the symbol.

■ Any ritual action has a "visceral" value. Communion, imposition of ashes, nailing written sins on a cross, a love feast, or even turning to a neighbor in the pew to reflect on the scripture just read are very meaningful acts that stick with us.

45

From *The Worship Workshop: Creative Ways to Design Worship Together,* by Marcia McFee. Copyright 2002 by Abingdon Press. Reproduced by permission.

CHAPTER 3

HOW CAN *History* HELP US CHANGE?

> *Have you ever heard this...?*
>
> "BUT WE'VE **ALWAYS** DONE IT THIS WAY!"

> In every age there were probably those who said, "But we've *always* done it this way!"

Caring for our rituals is a balancing act of the familiar and the new. Sometimes it is difficult to accept unfamiliar worship forms because it feels as if we are losing something along the way. And yet, lack of change or diversity can lead to a loss of passion for and interest in the call of the gospel to bring about the kingdom of God.

Often people use the argument, "It's so boring!" in response to claims that "We've always done it this way!" This continuous battle gets us nowhere. Perhaps it is boring because we've forgotten *why* we do it the way we do; perhaps we're just not aware of the vast practices that comprise the ways "we've done it." I believe that studying the history of worship can *help us make the changes necessary to revitalize worship* and get us past the age-old argument mentioned above.

The following interactive history tour traces a lineage of tradition, from worship in the Hebrew Bible (Old Testament) and early Christianity, through a mostly western-European trail, to Christian worship in America. The purpose of the tour is to note how forms change through time, rather than to give a comprehensive history lesson. Feel free to supplement the few notes included here with a text such as *A Brief History of Christian Worship* by James White.

WORSHIP HISTORY: A TRADITION OF CHANGE

On this journey all you need to bring is your imagination, a willingness to step temporarily into the shoes of other worshipers, and a keen eye for detail. Let's see if history can help us understand why change happens.

The gift of hindsight enables us to see that despite this plea, change happens. We are always responding to changing environments and social/cultural contexts. **Change occurs in**

order to keep the Story alive! What would have happened if the early Christians believed the *only* way to worship was as Miriam did at the Red Sea? In various periods of history, political and social circumstances have affected worship forms. And sometimes, changing cultural forms have changed the forms of worship expression. These are the things we must notice as we step through history and then direct ourselves on our own quest to determine what change is necessary in our day in order to continue to communicate the good news of God in our midst!

For each period of history, suggestions for an "interactive" experience are listed, based on my workshop experiences. Following these are hints for the leader that can help answer the questions listed below concerning environment, context, media, and participation. I suggest that the leader encourage the group to answer these, rather than simply read the included notes. It's likely that the group will come up with many more examples than the ones listed. Get creative with how you reenact these periods in history and **have fun!**

As you read each section, pay attention to the following:

> **The environment of worship: what influence does the environment have?**
>
> **The social/cultural context: what difference does the context make?**
>
> **The media of worship: what are the sights, sounds, and instruments?**
>
> **The participation in worship: how much participation is there and by whom?**

The Dance of Miriam: A Journeying People

One of the earliest examples in the Bible of the Israelite people worshiping is after they escape from Egypt and are successful in crossing the Red Sea. Miriam, as a ritual leader, is the one to stop and, along with the women (see Exodus 15:20-21), give praise to God in the way that is their custom in this time—by singing, dancing, drumming, and shouting!

"Then Moses and the Israelites sang this song to the LORD*:*

'I will sing to the LORD*, for he has triumphed gloriously;*
  horse and rider he has thrown into the sea.
The LORD *is my strength and my might,*
    and he has become my salvation;
this is my God, and I will praise him,
    my father's God, and I will exalt him. . . .
Pharaoh's chariots and his army he cast into the sea;
      his picked officers were sunk in the Red Sea.
The floods covered them;
        they went down into the depths like a stone. . . .
The enemy said, "I will pursue, I will overtake,
      I will divide the spoil, my desire shall have its fill of them.
      I will draw my sword, my hand shall destroy them."

You blew with your wind, the sea covered them;
*   they sank like lead in the mighty waters.*
Who is like you, O LORD, among the gods?
*   Who is like you, majestic in holiness,*
*   awesome in splendor, doing wonders? . . .*
In your steadfast love you led the people whom you redeemed;
*   you guided them by your strength to your holy abode.'"*
*   —Exodus 15:1-2, 4-5, 9-11, 13*

SUGGESTIONS

■ Worship outdoors, if possible, in a grassy area or the church parking lot!

■ All women gather in a circle with percussion instruments (or hand clapping) and process walking, skipping, or dancing around the circle, into the middle, and out again to a loud and steady rhythm.

■ Men read the Exodus text above (which was written later) *loudly* over the sounds of the women.

REFLECTIONS

environment: outside, lots of people, lots of noise, boisterous worship

context: "on the road," God goes with the people

media: drums, dancing, ecstatic nature, using only what they can carry

participation: women ritual leaders in the tradition of the Ancient Near East, high participation of people

God's House: Temple Worship

The Israelites now have their own land, their own power, and a new distinct way of worshiping. This psalm was probably sung during the annual ritual of the enthronement of the Lord when the ark was carried in procession into the temple. (Also see Exodus 30—added by priestly authors of the temple: altar, basin for water, sacred anointing oil, incense, lampstand; Exodus 31—commissioning of an artist.)

Psalm 132

[chime]
One: *O LORD, remember David and all the hardships he endured.*

[chime]
One: *He swore an oath to the LORD and made a vow to the Mighty One of Jacob:*
*   "I will not enter my house*
*   or go to my bed—*
*   I will allow no sleep to my eyes,*
*   no slumber to my eyelids,*
*   till I find a place for the LORD,*
*   a dwelling for the Mighty One of Jacob."*

[chime]
All: *We heard it in Ephrathah, we came upon it in the fields of Jaar:*
[candle and incense bearers process to altar]
*   "Let us go to his dwelling place; let us worship at his footstool—*
[chime, ark enters]
*   arise, O LORD, and come to your resting place, you and the ark of your might.*
[robe bearer processes]
*   May your priests be clothed with righteousness;*
*   may your saints sing for joy."*

[chime three times]
[King enters, is robed and sits next to the altar]
One: *For the sake of David your servant,*
*   do not reject your anointed one.*

*   The LORD swore an oath to David, a sure oath that he will not revoke:*
*   "One of your own descendants*
*   I will place on your throne—*
*   if your sons keep my covenant and the statutes I teach them, then their sons will sit*
*   on your throne for ever and ever."*
[set ark down center]

All: *For the LORD has chosen Zion, he has desired it for his dwelling:*

King: *"This is my resting place for ever and ever;*
*   here I will sit enthroned, for I have desired it—*
*   I will bless her with abundant provisions;*
*   her poor will I satisfy with food.*
*   I will clothe her priests with salvation,*
*   and her saints will ever sing for joy."*

[chime]
One: *"Here I will make a horn grow for David and set up a lamp for my anointed one.*
*   I will clothe his enemies with shame,*
*   but the crown on his head will be resplendent."*

[chime three times]
—from Psalm 132 (NIV)

SUGGESTIONS

■ Do this in the sanctuary.

■ Women stay in back providing "chime" sounds, either with bells, with chimes, or by singing "brrruuummmmmm."

■ Men divide into the following parts and prepare to process down main aisle at the times indicated in the text:
- "One" reader, standing at pulpit
- King
- candle bearer
- incense bearer (a jar of some kind)
- 2 ark bearers (a piano bench works well lifted above heads)
- robe bearer (a robe or purple cloth)
- other men, reading "All" parts.

REFLECTIONS

environment: indoors; liturgy more complex and ordered, written

context: seat of power and authority, King is God's representative, hierarchy

media: lots of "stuff" is used for ritual, no longer traveling, needed places to store objects used in ritual

participation: royalty, definitive roles, women have been replaced as keepers of ritual, those who know "the ritual" lead

The Diaspora: Exile and Lament

The beloved Temple is destroyed and the people are exiled to another land (the Babylonian exile). One result is a flourish of creativity as the people express their sorrow. The Psalms of Lament make up over half of the book of Psalms. Although these psalms express great pain, most of them also end with a word of hope to sustain the people and an expression of great faith that God will deliver them.

Psalm 137:1-3

By the rivers of Babylon—there we sat down and there we wept when we remembered Zion.
On the willows there we hung up our harps.
For there our captors asked us for songs,
and our tormentors asked for mirth, saying,
"Sing us one of the songs of Zion!"

Psalm 77:1

I cry aloud to God, aloud to God, that [God] may hear me.

SUGGESTIONS

- Process out of the sanctuary silently into nave.

- Lay down any musical instruments.

- Read Psalms of Lament.

REFLECTIONS

environment: people scattered, Temple is destroyed, living in foreign land

context: exiled, captive

media: must keep Story alive away from centralized place; "songs of Zion" remembered, handed on

participation: those who remember, have, know the rituals, the Story

Around the Table: Early Christianity

Three Jewish centers of worship are the foundation of Christian practice:

1 *Temple:* sacrificial offerings, picked up in language of Eucharistic prayer ("blood of the covenant, shed for many") as well as psalms in temple worship ("Blessed is he who comes in the name of the LORD."—Psalm 118:26 [NIV])

2 *Synagogue:* prayers, blessing God for what God has done

3 *Table:* origin of the Eucharistic prayer from the Jewish table prayers of blessing and thanksgiving (*berakoth*) and the thanksgiving said over the cup at the end of the meal (*birkat ha-mazon*). The *Didache* (third century text) is the earliest and clearest example of this:

> And after you have had your fill, give thanks thus:
>
> *"We give thanks to you, holy Father, for your holy Name which you have enshrined in our hearts, and for the knowledge and faith and immortality which you have made known to us through your child Jesus: glory to you for evermore.*
>
> *"You, almighty Master, created all things for the sake of your Name, and gave food and drink to humankind for their enjoyment, that they might*

give you thanks; but to us you have granted spiritual food and drink and eternal life through your child Jesus. Above all we give you thanks because you are mighty; glory to you for evermore. Amen."

Then later in the third century, from the oldest known Western form of the Eucharistic prayer (*Apostolic Tradition* by Hippolytus from Rome), the institution narrative is added:

And when he was betrayed to voluntary suffering that he might destroy death, and break the bonds of the devil, and tread down hell, and shine upon the righteous, and fix a term, and manifest the resurrection, he took bread and gave thanks to you, saying, "Take, eat; this is my body, which shall be broken for you." Likewise also the cup, saying "This is my blood, which is shed for you; when you do this, you make my remembrance."

SUGGESTIONS

- Sit in small groups around tables and imagine the food there (not just bread and wine).

- Have the eldest (male or female) in each group read the ancient texts.

- Reflect as a whole group.

REFLECTIONS

environment: house churches, small, intimate

context: secret, illegal activity, persecution

media: the common elements of sharing a meal (as ritualized by Jesus, this is remembered)

participation: all are fed, especially those who are poor, leadership by men and women

Water and the Spirit: Early Church Baptism

For candidates for baptism, there is a long (one source says three years!) catechumenate during which they cannot pray with, kiss, or remain for Eucharist with the faithful. As the season of Lent develops, it is a time of intense preparation for the catechumenates, including instruction and daily exorcism. In the three days before Easter (the *Triduum*) they fast in preparation for baptism.

Suggestions & Reflections

Then on Easter morning at cockcrow, ancient accounts tell us that some form of the following ritual happened:

- prayer is offered over the water
- candidates undress (men and women are in separate rooms)
- bishop prepares oils of exorcism and thanksgiving (called chrism)
- renunciations of Satan are spoken
- bishop breathes on the faces of the candidates (to recall the breath of God at creation)
- candidates are anointed thoroughly with oil of exorcism (a coarse, gritty oil)
- candidates and deacon(ess) go into the water
- candidates are asked three questions ("Do you believe?")
- they are immersed after each affirmation of the Trinity (3 times)
- they are anointed with the oil of thanksgiving (a fine, scented oil)
- each candidate dresses in white
- they process with a candle to the waiting church body (which has been praying all this time)
- bishop blesses with the sign of the cross on the forehead with holy oil
- bishop gives kiss of peace
- first prayer with congregation is offered (Lord's Prayer)
- the body of worshipers gives kiss of peace
- all participate in celebrating the Eucharist (three cups: water, milk and honey, wine)

SUGGESTIONS

- Go into a dark room.

- Have one volunteer stand with lit candle to represent candidate for baptism.

- Describe the process of the baptismal ritual.

- Recite the Lord's Prayer at the appropriate time.

[After reflecting together, this is a good time to take a break.]

REFLECTIONS

environment: intimate, private (deaconess attends women)

context: secret, illegal activity, many give up professions and family to become a Christian

media: lots of symbolism, need for strong and memorable ritual

participation: whole body prays, church is forming roles

Suggestions & Reflections

Out of the Closet: Fourth-Century Worship

Legalization of Christianity: The Fourth Century

THE CLASSIC PERIOD (300–600)

With the legalization of Christianity in the fourth century, many changes occur in worship. As a state religion, there are now large numbers of people to accommodate. The church has money and political power, and just look what happens—

- churches are built to look like the courts ("basilicas")
- worship takes on a "courtly" character
- priests begin to wear robes (like the court!)
- worship texts are more and more "set"
- processions of people going to church parade in the street
- much more singing develops to give time for all this parading of things
- daily morning and evening prayer services develop as well as the monastic life of constant praying and worshiping

Suggestions & Reflections

SUGGESTIONS

- Process up and down a hall in the church singing or shouting loudly, "This is the day the Lord has made; let us rejoice and be glad in it!"

REFLECTIONS

environment: big buildings to hold the many Christian "converts"

context: legal, state religion, correlation to imperial court

media: lots of "show," elaborate ritual

participation: "officials" (church and state) lead, grand processions bring the masses into the church

Separation Anxiety: The Medieval Church

MEDIEVAL PERIOD (600–1500)

Although worship is rich and full, the people get further from the action of the ritual in this time period. Churches get bigger and longer (think of large cathedrals) with the altar table and what happens there more secretive and off-limits. Eventually, most people "commune" by gazing upon the lifted host (i.e., the bread wafer) at the appropriate moment (a bell would ring to let you know when that was happening). In addition, the times were characterized by

- separation of clergy and people
- worship texts and actions that reflect "right" thinking lots of controversy over what, exactly, is "right" thinking
- the people developing their own piety—their own rituals since much of the liturgy didn't involve them directly:
     praying with a rosary
     running from church to church to see more than one host
     praying at altars of the relics of the saints or the reserved host
     folk dancing in the nave!

SUGGESTIONS

- Have a clergyperson lift a wafer or piece of bread at the altar and ring a bell to reenact the "high" point of the liturgy.

- Do a folk dance in the main aisle (for example, try a simple round dance to "God Rest Ye Merry, Gentlefolk").

REFLECTIONS

environment: "holy" places not accessible to the people

context: great separation between those in power and the masses

media: visuals stressed, cathedral architecture

participation: clergy do "right" ritual, the people devise their own!

Forming and Reforming: The Beginnings of Protestant Worship

REFORMATION (1500s)

Spurred by such things as the invention of the printing press, the more available study of humanities and languages (a growing focus on words), and the desire for more active participation of the people, Luther, Calvin, Zwingli, and other "reformers" call for a different way to know and experience God. The results were diverse but here are some examples:
- more focus on preaching (and understanding) the Word
- worship and Bibles are changed from Latin (which the people didn't speak anymore) to their own languages
- elaborate ceremony and visual art decreases (some reformers eliminated it altogether)
- hymnody sung by the people as well as polyphonic music (Calvin wanted only simple long and short note singing)
- the people are allowed to partake of the bread and cup for communion

SUGGESTIONS

■ Gather around the pulpit to reflect on this section.

■ Read a short paragraph of scripture and imagine hearing it in your own language for the first time.

REFLECTIONS

environment: the Word is valued over visuals

context: reaction against Catholicism

media: arts and ceremony suffer; reading, speaking, and comprehending heightened

participation: people can comprehend words of the liturgy and actively partake of communion

The Age of Reason: Enlightenment

ENLIGHTENMENT (1700s)

"Have courage to use your own reason!" is the motto for this era. Mystery and miracles are suspicious and authority is questioned. Words that "make sense" and that can be grasped by the mind are valued above all else. What does this mean for worship?

■ services reflect sacramental minimalism

■ Protestant churches continue to emphasize preaching and speaking the Word

■ Catholic churches become more and more ornate, drawing attention away from the liturgy itself

■ value of sign-acts decreases (baptismal fonts get so small that they can fit on a pedestal)

SUGGESTIONS

■ Gather around the baptismal font to reflect on this section.

■ Look around at the arrangement of your sanctuary. Is it influenced by this era?

REFLECTIONS

environment: preaching churches are built with pulpit central; minimalism

context: age of much intellectual/industrial advancement; mind valued

media: less symbolism and action in ritual

participation: individual reason valued

Early America Worships: The Frontier

CAMP MEETINGS (1800s)

People on the frontier have to travel great distances to come together for worship. They aren't about to stop the movement once they get there! In worship, it is important for them to "move" literally and spiritually:

- conversion is the goal
- emotional preaching and testimonials are heard
- altar calls are frequent
- ecstatic, demonstrative, uninhibited expression is possible
- simple, repetitive singing accommodates illiteracy and lack of books

SUGGESTIONS

- Sit in pews.

- Sing "Blessed Be the Name of the Lord," clapping hands and stomping feet.

REFLECTIONS

environment: loud, boisterous, lots of energy

context: time also for socializing, release from stress of hard lives

media: simple, no songbooks, few people read

participation: high, personal conversion valued

Early America Worships: The City

WEALTHY, URBAN CENTERS (1800s)

In the city centers, patterns of worship are emerging which would be described as "more respectable." There is an appeal to "good taste," to a sense of beauty and order. The emphasis is on giving God "our best." Here is what develops:

- trained musicians take over some of the singing
- organs become popular as the "sacred instrument"
- more elaborate ceremony develops (more stuff with more money!) such as robes for the choir and acolytes
- hymnbooks like *Hymns Ancient and Modern, 1861,* allow more complicated hymnody, musically and theologically
- participation from the people is more "dignified" or static than that of the camp meeting

SUGGESTIONS

■ Sing "Holy, Holy, Holy" (with organ—no dancing around!).

REFLECTIONS

environment: inside, liturgy more complex, printed materials

context: wealthier, educated

media: more "stuff" of ritual—organs, robes, candlesticks, paraments can be afforded

participation: professionals take on responsibility to "give God our best"

Early America Worships: The Invisible Church

The invisible church is the slave church. Often their worship is done under the cloak of secrecy, in fields or at night. Slaves in some areas also worship in the white churches but in segregated sections. The invisible church, however, is a place where the unique forms, songs, and theology of the exiled Africans could be freely expressed. Here are just some of the forms it takes:

■ songs sung during work by day would contain "codes" for the time and place of the meeting at night
■ quilts and blankets hung from trees around the community were saturated with water to soak up the sound
■ the community gathered around iron pots to "catch" the sounds, singing softly, heads huddled together
■ singing and speaking took the form of call and response
■ "ring shout" dances develop

SUGGESTIONS

■ Gather in a huddle in the main aisle.

■ Lean heads together, sing a spiritual softly, slowly (for example, "Nobody Knows the Trouble I've Seen").

REFLECTIONS

environment: often outside, houses, barns, at night, intimate

context: illegal in most cases, secret, fear of persecution

media: rituals and songs gleaned and created from life experiences and scripture

participation: elders pass on Story and ritual

HANDOUT

> **HMMM . . . SOUND FAMILIAR?**
> compare notes in the following sections:
> - A Journeying People (p. 47) & The Frontier (p. 57)
> - Temple Worship (p. 48) & The City (p. 57)
> - Early Christianity (p. 51) & The Invisible Church (p. 58)

> **HMMM . . . A THOUGHT:**
> "Reformation" happened when the people were separated from meaningful ritual (p. 55).
> - What does this teach us about the importance of "the work of the people" in our time?

Here We Are: The Twenty-First Century!

We are a result of rich and diverse worship practices handed down through the ages. As we have seen, it is the form of worship that changed in order to keep the Story alive in vastly different environments and situations. After you have taken "the tour," reflect on our own environment and context and how it affects the way we worship. Use the questions below to guide your discussion, or simply start talking about what you discovered, what you think is important to learn from this, and what history has to teach us about handing the Story on to the next generations.

- What difference does our environment make to our worship forms?

- What is our social/cultural/political context? Is it having an effect on us?

- What media are available to communicate God's love to us and to the world?

- How do we participate in our worship? Who participates?

- Are our worship forms meaningful and memorable to us and to the next generation?

Our worship must be BOTH *"traditional"* **AND** *"contemporary"*

"TRADITION" = *to hand on, to surrender*

"CONTEMPORARY" = *all we have been,*
all we are,
all we hope to be

> Diverse worship draws on the past, pays attention to the present, and never fails to dream of a better future with hope in God.

59

THE WORSHIP WORKSHOP

CHAPTER 4

GET MORE PEOPLE INVOLVED USING SEASONAL *Teams*

I lived in New York City for many years and was a member of a large United Methodist church there. I was a part of the worship committee. We would meet in the chairperson's apartment, have some fabulous snacks, and, for the most part, talk about whether we should get some new paraments or if we needed to recruit more ushers. Many worship committees function like this, essentially as "stewards" of the worship duties. These are important things; however, my hope is that worship committees or teams, and certainly your worship staff, are more integrally involved in creating diverse ways to present the good news in worship—in other words, **DESIGNING WORSHIP.**

A Seasonal Team Model

There are several ways of going about getting more people involved. I have developed **a model for seasonal design teams.** Although no one model is the answer for everyone, you can take some of the suggestions included here and adapt them to your best use (see page 75 for some ideas for adaptation). The important thing is to find the model that generates the most energy and excitement from the people and spreads the responsibilities to many.

HERE IS THE IDEA:

Extended group: open invitation
Seasonal team: volunteers
Core team: staff and worship committee year round
involved in one season
involved in one "party"

CORE TEAM: This is a team made of the clergy and staff of the church, including musicians (full and/or part time) as well as a worship "committee" that you may already have established. If you don't, the staff comprises this team. Or if you have persons who take care of "stewarding" worship stuff—like ushers and elements and greeters—by all means continue to use them in this very important role. However, there may be some changes in the kind of things that they deal with. For example, a group that takes care of recruiting ushers may be asked to find multigenerational ushers for a certain season. Or a group that has been taking care of paraments on the table may be asked to help with visuals that aren't "the usual." It is vitally important that they are on board early in the creative process so that they don't feel "left out."

This core team's job is to provide continuity from season to season, shepherd the process, and act as an editor when it gets down to final decisions. This team works year round.

SEASONAL TEAM: This team comprises people who would like to work on one liturgical season. This model is based on the fact that most people don't have time to serve on a year-round committee. Our lives are full, but they often have ebbs and flows of rush and rest. Some people may be able to help out during the fall on an Advent Team; some people are more likely to have time in the winter/spring to work on a Lent Team. This team should be no less than eight people (unless you are a very small church).

This team's job is to supplement the core team to plan and then implement one liturgical season. They may be "behind the scenes" or part of worship leadership, or they may recruit others for certain pieces.

EXTENDED TEAM: This team comprises people who answer an open invitation to party! There can be as many as your space (I suggest someone's house, not the church) will hold. The first meeting of a seasonal team is a fun time of brainstorming and learning about the season. It is a time to hear lots of thoughts and ideas about the season and possibly identify an emerging theme.

This team's job is to spend one evening with the core and seasonal teams giving input to discussion about the season, the scriptures, and the focus for that season. They are not asked to continue with specific jobs but some may volunteer to help if asked later in the process.

So, imagine this: By the time the liturgical season rolls around, the number of people who are excited about it and anticipating it could exceed several dozen!

Staff—don't panic yet: It may feel like a lot of cooks in the kitchen, and you may be thinking, "wouldn't it just be easier to do it myself?" Once the wheels get oiled and you have some experience with this style of planning, it actually becomes easier and more energizing. Besides, is doing it all yourself the faithful thing to do with **"the work of the people"**?

TEAM TIME LINE!

The liturgical year can be broken down into these seasons (and thus, these teams):

Advent—the four Sundays before Christmas (could also include Christmas Eve)**

Christmas/Epiphany—from Christmas to the beginning of Lent

Lent—the six weeks before Easter**

Holy Week—this could be handled by the Lent team but there could also be a different team if there are several services

Easter Season—from Easter Sunday to Pentecost

Season After Pentecost / Ordinary Time—until Advent (can be two or three different chunks)**

** <u>Note:</u> Do not attempt to do all of these in the beginning. Instead I recommend starting with an Advent team. Then follow that with a Lent team and one summer season team. Gradual change will allow time to evaluate the process between seasons and alleviate the staff from having to work simultaneously with more than one team. Moreover, it gives everyone an opportunity to learn and adapt to a new style of design and leadership.

When do we start?

HERE IS A SUGGESTED TIME LINE:

8 weeks before the season starts
- ■ Brainstorming party!

6 weeks before the season starts
- ■ Seasonal team interest groups report back with ideas
- ■ Some editing decisions made

4 weeks before the season starts
- ■ First drafts of services completed
- ■ Organizational tasks and needs identified

2 weeks before the season starts
- ■ Check in with interest groups
- ■ Finalize tasks
- ■ Get extra help where it is needed

Of course, there can be many variations on this time line that can condense or extend it. However, *never* start this process later than 6 weeks before the season starts. **The goal here is to allow the experience to be one of spiritual growth for the people involved, rather than stress and rush.**

HOW TO GO ABOUT IT

STEP ONE Get the support of the staff and existing worship team members by studying this workbook together. Have your own congregational "Worship Workshop," and take note of persons who have a high interest and passion for being more involved.

STEP TWO For the first attempt, handpick a Seasonal Team who will be excited about contributing to the process. Invite them to a staff or team meeting to learn more about the process.

STEP THREE Get out your calendars and the Team Time Line (page 62), and schedule meetings for the whole process. It will look like a lot of work. Just remember that it is also a lot of fun!

STEP FOUR Create a flyer or bulletin insert inviting people to the Brainstorming Party. Use language that affirms "liturgy" as the "work of the people" and that affirms our God-given creativity. Everyone Is Creative on page 64 will give you some good ideas for the flyer. Make sure you "bill" the evening as fun and interactive (a party) and not as a typical meeting. One way of ensuring participation is to ask the Seasonal and Core Team members to invite someone to come with them.

STEP FIVE Have the brainstorming party! Use the instructions on pages 65 (Brainstorming Party) through 68 (Human Thesaurus) to help you plan this. You need not end up with an agreed-upon theme at this party. Don't let the evening get bogged down with decision making. The brainstorming part of the party should take no more than an hour (of course, eating and fellowship afterwards can be open-ended).

STEP SIX Follow up immediately with a Seasonal/Core Team gathering in order to identify a theme (p. 69), cross-reference scripture (p. 70), and identify interest groups (p. 71) for the next step in the process.

STEP SEVEN Continue to follow the Team Time Line using Putting It on Paper (p. 73) and Worship Rough Drafts Checklist (p. 74) to help you with the final stages of the process.

STEP EIGHT Fine tune details as you work on the performance aspects of the worship services using Worship Leadership Skills (p. 77) and The Language of Leadership (p. 78) to help you.

EVERYONE IS CREATIVE

We are all creative by virtue of having been created in the image of God! We have erroneously come to identify "creative" people as those who are artistically inclined. But we all create in some way every day of our lives. Creativity is a way of being. When we open our eyes to the possibility that every moment is filled with the miracle of life and newness, we live in hope. To be creative is to dare to believe that God could bring about more than we can "think or imagine."

I believe that we can "exercise" our creative abilities and learn to be more creative by doing some simple things. A special PBS presentation on creativity outlined four powerful tools to develop your own creativity:

FAITH IN YOUR OWN CREATIVITY

Start noticing the evidence of creativity already in your life.

ABSENCE OF JUDGMENT

Don't let the voice of judgment inside of you censor your ideas before you have a chance to develop them.

PRECISE OBSERVATION

Look at the world with the wonder of a child and the precision of a scientist; this outlook will give you a new sense of awareness.

PENETRATING QUESTIONS

Nurture an insatiable curiosity; it will reward you with endless possibilities!

"Holy play invites us to a profound trust that God has created us to delight in the gift of life."

—Don Saliers, *Worship Come to Its Senses*

BRAINSTORMING PARTY!

Now that we have affirmed that we are all creative, it's time to party!

This is the first step to the team design model described on the previous pages. There is an open invitation to the congregation to sign up to come to a seasonal design team "Brainstorming Party!" I recommend having it at someone's home rather than at the church simply because people often feel freer to have fun and think "outside the box" when we aren't in the church space. Oh—and have food!

Set up a flip chart or paper on a wall and markers where someone can write the brainstorm lists so everyone can see. Here are my suggested steps. Again, always feel free to adapt and improvise!

■ After you have gathered and helped yourselves to something to eat and drink, take ten minutes to talk about the season. An excellent guide is *The New Handbook of the Christian Year*. We can't assume that everyone knows what "Advent," for example, represents. Don't make this long or like a lecture—we don't want to kill the creative atmosphere.

■ Have everyone pair up and spend one minute each chatting about something unrelated and easy to talk about (like "what I did today"). This is an exercise just to get everyone comfortable with talking out loud.

■ Write the name of the season at the top of the poster board or flip chart. Go over the "IRIS" rules about brainstorming on page 66. Let people know that you can use words that relate to the season or you can play off of words that someone else shouts out (for instance, if you hear "purple" and think "people-eater," go ahead and say it!). Then let 'em loose, encouraging everyone to shout out words that come to their heads "popcorn" style. Brainstorm until you have at least 20 words. Then try some of the other creative exercises on the following pages, including the cross-referencing scripture exercise.

■ Demonstrate the process called "Random Stimulation" on p. 67. Then have folks pair up to pick two words of their own from the list and explore the connections. Let them work for 5-10 minutes on this. If some pairs finish before others, invite them to pick two more words. Then call the group back together to share these "seeds" of ideas for a theme and focus for the season. This will take about 10 to 15 minutes to accomplish.

■ Demonstrate the exercise called "Human Thesaurus" on p. 68. Have the same partners use their words (or pick others) to come up with more ideas and then report back to the whole group any new ideas which emerge. Let this process take less than 10 minutes.

■ Take the last 5 minutes to get feedback on context. Make a list of answers to this question: "What has happened in our world, in our community, and in our church that makes the celebration of this season different from any other time in our history?"

■ The whole process should take about an hour unless there is a lot of energy and people want to take more time. Stop before everyone gets really tired and enjoy other conversation and food. Afterwards, have the core and seasonal teams meet to compare notes and begin to identify a theme. Make sure you keep track of who was a part of the "Extended Team" so that they can be thanked in a newsletter or bulletin during the season.

Note: Let many ideas come forth. Don't get stuck too long on the first idea that comes up—or even the next idea. The best idea is not always the first one. Don't discount "wild" ideas. It may be that a solid, doable idea will spring from it. Have core team members look for "energy surges." These are times when an idea is presented and there is a lot of energy from the group around it. You are looking for ideas that carry excitement, depth, and relevance.

IRIS

Steering through the "eye" of the brainstorm
CO-CREATING WITH OTHERS

I = IMPULSIVELY IDENTIFY IDEAS
- Use a "popcorn" style of feedback with the person recording the words writing as quickly as possible; this helps the energy stay high and keeps people from "thinking" too much!

R = RELAX AND RESERVE REACTIONS
- Accept all ideas. Hold back judgments until after the brainstorm process and write down all offerings.

I = INCLUDE, INTERACT WITH, AND INCORPORATE THE IDEAS OF OTHERS
- Fuse and feed off of each other's ideas to make new ideas.

S = SAMPLE STRANGE AND SEEMINGLY SILLY IDEAS
- Novel, unusual, different, and original ideas are encouraged. Ideas that segue to other interests and concerns help expand possibilities.

RANDOM STIMULATION: A CREATIVE PROCESS

Edward de Bono's creative process called "random stimulation" has helped me to think of ideas that I would never have thought of without it. He writes that we are unlikely to restructure our patterns of thinking if we always work from already established patterns. Our brains like to think in patterns. We like to think about what we know. Random stimulation is a technique to put two seemingly dissimilar things together to spark a new idea. Here's how this method works in a brainstorming session:

Ask two people to pick a number between 1 and 20 (or however many words you have in your brainstorm list). Then count either from the top or bottom (or any which way—just so that the leader is not subconsciously picking the two words) and circle those two words. Explore the relationship between them and allow this to spark another idea. For example, here is a brainstormed list of words for Advent:

ADVENT

waiting	message
expectation	e-mail
pregnant	voice mail
carry	star
journey	radiant
child	glowing
manger	follow
stink	followers
preparation	visitors
census	homage
count	gifts
families	purple
controversy	people-eater
unwed	candles
angel	greenery

So, imagine that the words "preparation" and "e-mail" were randomly picked. A discussion about their connection might go like this: "I see a theme of 'how we are preparing for newness in our lives.' Reminders of God's possibilities abound but are we 'on-line' to receive them? Are our eyes open? I could see a focus on spiritual practices during the season: prayer, devotion, journaling. We could have e-mail and website emphasis in our evangelism for the season, and for mission we could 'send a message of God's presence' by our presence at homeless shelters and food lines." See how this works? The combination of the two words sparks an idea.

67

HUMAN THESAURUS: DIGGING DEEPER

After you have done the "random stimulation" exercise, take the two words that have been circled and discussed, and place them at the top of a piece of paper. Underneath each, make a list of other ways to say each previous word (like a thesaurus). In other words, in the example below, the words listed don't all rename the word "preparation," they ask this question: "What's another way to say _____?" So it goes like this:

PREPARATION

(what's another way to say "preparation"?)
GET READY

(what's another way to say "get ready"?)
AWARE

(what's another way to say "aware"?)
LOOK

(you get the idea!)

Do each word separately. Here's an example:

PREPARATION	E-MAIL
get ready	instant message
aware	immediate
look	now
watch	timely
observe	relevant
notice	newsworthy
pay attention	information
awake	knowledge
alive ←——————————→	known
lively	identity

Now, cross-reference the two lists in several ways, again combining words to see what other ideas may spark. For instance, to be **known** is to feel **alive**. Who are the people in our community who are lonely, feeling isolated and unknown? The birth of the Christ Child in a lowly stable reminds us that the holy resides everywhere. What is the church's response?

Try other combinations. What is interesting is that the words themselves may never show up after the initial brainstorming party, but they will have been catalysts for new ideas.

IDENTIFYING A THEME

There needn't be a definitive answer regarding a theme at the brainstorming party. There may be one that just naturally seems to have consensus, but if not don't push it. The Seasonal and Core Teams now must hone down the possibilities and make a decision. This is often easier in a smaller group.

Was there any topic that brought about a great deal of energy from the group?

Spend some time together as a team sharing personal witness of this good news. This helps us integrate our upcoming work with our personal experience.
"My faith has helped me know about

_____ when...
(theme)

Were there brainstormed ideas from different groups that were similar?

_____

_____."

Can you construct a simple statement, considering the emerging theme and the contextual information expressed by the extended team, of the good news that needs to be heard and shared with this community right now?
(e.g., "God is always with us.")

If you do not follow the lectionary and have not already chosen scripture, it is time! At this point, we begin to see what the scriptures will say to us this season. If you do follow the lectionary or when you have identified the scriptures to be used in the season, continue to the "Cross-Referencing Scripture" exercise.

What does our faith tell us about the emerging topic/theme?

Can you begin to identify a theme and perhaps sub-themes to differentiate each Sunday of the season? (e.g., theme—"Being There"; four Sundays of Advent—"The Promise," "The Prophecy," "The Process," "The Presence")

What scriptures address this theme?

CROSS-REFERENCING SCRIPTURE

The reason I prefer to brainstorm ideas before looking at scripture is that when we get tied into the text immediately, we are less likely to come up with something that hasn't been done before. It has been my experience that one or more of the ideas that come out of the previous exercises will work in concert with the scriptures once they are explored, especially since the editors of the lectionary had the theology of the season in mind as they made decisions. Of course, one year you may want to adapt the process to have a Bible study group study the scriptures and bring their thoughts to the Extended Team at the brainstorming party. The following process is based on using the lectionary. However, if you are a preacher who wants to work with specific texts that you choose, you can use this format, substituting your selections.

Here is what I suggest:

■ Divide into four groups. One group will look at the scriptures from the **Hebrew Bible** (Old Testament) for the whole season; another will look at the **Psalm** selections; the third group will read the **Epistle** lessons; and the fourth will take a look at the **Gospel** readings. The reason for this arrangement (instead of having each group look at all the readings for one Sunday) is so that we can get an idea of the development within the particular book used and begin to see a journey from one Sunday to the next, rather than as completely separate services. This approach helps us develop the season as a whole.

■ Have copies available for each person in each group with their readings. In each group, have individuals read the scripture while everyone circles words on their paper that "pop out" at them—that catch their attention, intrigue them or just seem alive to them. After reading one scripture, make a master list of words that people circled, noting the most "popular" ones.

■ Have the group complete this process for each one of the Sundays' readings, and place the group's master lists side by side. Have them look at their group's lists. Is there a common theme or message? Is there a progression of ideas? Does something particular emerge? Come up with a description of your observations that you can report back to the whole group.

■ Have each group report back. Begin to discuss how these things seem to "dance" with some of the ideas that came out of the seasonal "brainstorm." Does something emerge that seems to be particularly meaningful and relevant for this time and place and people?

IDENTIFYING INTEREST GROUPS

At this point in the process, it is time to identify interest groups within the seasonal team that will begin to gather resources for the services. Their first meeting time together will be a compiling of resources without making final editing decisions. It is their responsibility to bring back some concrete ideas to the whole team but be flexible enough to alter their ideas. It is important for them to realize that once each interest group reports back, some decisions will have to be made to blend them into a cohesive whole. And it may be that another group's information will spark an even better idea. Or it may be that too many good ideas will be presented and some paring down will be necessary.

Examples of Interest Groups

Here are some suggested interest groups and comments about them:

MUSIC

This interest group will be made up of music staff and others from the seasonal team. It is good to get a mixture of people. For instance, it is good to have both someone who has musical proficiency and someone who loves music but might not be very musically inclined (this is a way of testing out new songs that would be easy for everyone to learn). Also, it would be good to try not to have people who all prefer only one style of music. There should be a clear commitment to diversity of music and attention to well-grounded theology in picking hymns and songs.

VISUALS

This interest group can include people who have some talent in the visual arts, but it is not necessary. Persons with the kind of "spatial intelligence" described in Gardner's "Multiple Intelligence Theory" (pages 37-38) are great for this group. It may involve people who like to rearrange furniture, collect candles, or enjoy decorating their houses and changing table centerpieces. The idea is that these people have a commitment to "seeing" the Story told.

WRITING

This interest group will begin to collect already-written materials that help express the theme and to write or commission people to write liturgies and prayers. This group should include those who love to read, look through books, or journal and write. You may want to incorporate part of the ministerial staff in this group.

DRAMATIZING

This group pays attention to the "visceral" stuff. The preacher(s) should be in close contact with this group so as to point them toward the focus of the sermon. It is important that the word "dramatizing" not be narrowed only to mean "putting on skits." This group will take a look at scriptures and see which ones would be good to *dramatize* (as we have described—using unusual placement of readers, many voices, music or hymn interspersed). If you have access to dancers, this team may decide what Sunday would be most appropriate to include them. This team also looks at the "response to the Word." What ritual actions can we *do* to embody the Word? This will include communion, interacting with the visuals (in collaboration with the visual group) and any other kind of "call to action" (in collaboration with the action response group).

IDENTIFYING INTEREST GROUPS (CONTINUED)

ACTION RESPONSE

This interest group takes a look at how what happens in worship can also be emphasized in the rest of the life of the church. For example, they may ask Sunday school teachers to also use the theme and focus in their curriculum for the season. They may suggest ways that the congregation can be called to a particular mission focus for the season. They will talk about how to "get the word out" to the community (you can call it "publicity" or "evangelism!") and they may decide to call the church to form special small groups for spiritual formation, support, and/or fellowship during the season. They would be the group to organize something like a devotional booklet or prayer vigil of some kind. This group should be made up of people who have a history of being or a desire to be a part of programs outside of worship. Staff and core team members to consult with this group would be those involved in the ministries mentioned above.

How Do These Fit into the Time Line?

After the brainstorming party and the decision for a focus/theme (**eight weeks** before the season starts), interest groups meet on their own (possibly **seven weeks** before). They bring ideas and resources, and create or look for more at their meeting.

The interest groups report back with this plethora of ideas to the whole Seasonal Team at the next meeting (**six weeks** before). At this time, the whole team makes some editing decisions and gives guidance for the continuing work of the interest groups.

Before the next Seasonal Team meeting (**four weeks** before), the Interest Groups hone their ideas and produce drafts that are collected by the staff for compilation. The goal is for the staff to have rough drafts of the services for the next meeting. At that meeting (**four weeks** before), these rough drafts are discussed and organizational tasks and needs are identified and begun (any rehearsals planned, any mission tasks organized, any devotions for a booklet compiled, and so forth).

The final meeting of the Seasonal Team (**two weeks** before the start of the season) is a check-in with those who have been assigned tasks. If extra energy and hands are needed for any particular tasks, those who have less to do can volunteer to help. At this meeting it is important to identify what organizational and leadership help will be needed before, during, and after the services. Teamwork does not end with the creative and design process! Hands and hearts are needed throughout the season!

And last but not least, celebrate and give thanks for the teamwork, the fellowship, and the resulting worship of God!

Note: _Throughout this process, pastors and staff are shepherds of the process—giving room for grassroots ideas to flourish, and guiding and editing in the final stages. There is a point at which staff can help the process by discerning and naming the direction of the group._

PUTTING IT ON PAPER

We Gather
(calling to worship, greeting, singing)

We Proclaim God's Word
(praying, reading litanies, singing, reading scripture, proclaiming, giving testimony)

We Respond
(praying, celebrating communion or participating in other actions to "practice what we preach," committing to action, singing, giving offerings)

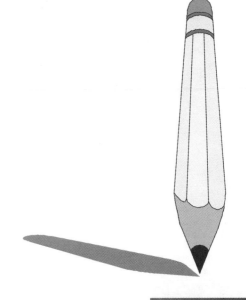

We Go into the World
(blessing one another, singing, going out)

From *The Worship Workshop: Creative Ways to Design Worship Together,* by Marcia McFee. Copyright 2002 by Abingdon Press. Reproduced by permission.

WORSHIP ROUGH DRAFTS CHECKLIST

✔ There is a balance of familiar and new

✔ There is a balance of community interaction and personal reflection

✔ Many voices are heard

✔ The story is told in many ways (words, visuals, actions)

✔ The language has depth—it is interesting, understandable, and inclusive

✔ The theme is woven throughout the service

✔ There is a nice flow of dynamics
(not monotonous—a balance of energetic and calm time)

From *The Worship Workshop: Creative Ways to Design Worship Together*, by Marcia McFee. Copyright 2002 by Abingdon Press. Reproduced by permission.

ADAPTATIONS TO THE SEASONAL MODEL

Here are some ideas about getting more people involved in planning worship. Add your own!

The following ideas have been generated by my work with congregations who have created diverse ways to implement the seasonal team model. Whatever the format you choose or create, the point is to get more people involved in the work of worship design. Add your own ideas to the list!

■ Develop the process in incremental steps by starting with an Extended Team brainstorming party only. The persons currently responsible for designing worship use this evening as fodder for their work. Once you are accustomed to the added input and people have gotten excited about the fun of "helping out," add the Seasonal Team concept.

■ If you have several services (of different or similar styles), use the same Extended Team brainstorming party as fodder for all of them. What a wonderful opportunity for people of the same church who don't get to worship together to work together on something that will feed the whole church, even if the end results vary widely in expression!

■ Use already existing small groups to help carry out the design process for a season. This becomes their curriculum for 6 weeks. (See next page.)

■ Use a work area or committee (finance, stewardship, mission, education, pastor relations) to prepare one service as a way of increasing their fellowship and connection to the worship life of the church.

■ Create an on-going group of people who like to write to create prayers, litanies, and poems for upcoming seasons.

■ Make a habit of using the people themselves as resources for visuals such as candles, cups, pitchers, plates, vases, fountains, plants, and artwork.

■ Create a Bible study group that meets with the staff and worship committee to study and discuss the lectionary readings for the upcoming season.

PLANNING WORSHIP WITH EXISTING SMALL GROUPS

The following offers another way of getting more people involved in worship planning. Consider using a Sunday school class or a weekly discipleship group. Planning worship involves Bible study, study of the Christian liturgical year, theologizing, prayer, and fellowship. What a great way to enhance a group's experience together.

Discuss...

Week 1: Meet together as a whole group to learn about and discuss the season, its theology, and its history. Talk about what expectations and practices your particular congregation has and discuss them in light of what you have learned about the season. What new revelations does the group have about the focus of the season?

Study...

Week 2: Divide into smaller groups for Bible study of the lectionary readings for the season (I would advise assigning the groups to "The First Lessons," "The Psalms," "The Gospels," and so forth, rather than to all the readings of one particular Sunday so that they can also focus on the particular book and author). If your congregation does not use the lectionary, the pastor and staff should prepare the list of readings for each Sunday for study.

Brainstorm...

Week 3: Have the groups report back to the larger group, sharing important topics of conversation, themes, or ideas that came out of their study. Compare and contrast these and begin to look for a focus that could develop throughout the season. Have members look for resources about the theme during the week.

Gather Ideas...

Week 4-5: Once a core idea has emerged, divide again into smaller interest groups (and get other members who would be assets involved) and begin to flesh out ways to proclaim the Word. (See "Identifying Interest Groups" on page 72.)

Plan...

Week 6: Gather as a whole to share more specific ideas related to the focus that arose in the interest groups. At this point, the brainstorming and information gathering parts of the creative process are drawing to a close. It is at this point that the pastor and staff become a guide for the editing process. Dedication to the gospel proclaimed, simplicity, meaning, and effective communication become the criteria. Tasks are assigned and God's people proceed to do the work of the worshiping community!

Worship!

WORSHIP LEADERSHIP SKILLS

Our goal is to use more people in worship leadership roles. This affirms that everyone is empowered to proclaim God's glory and God's presence. We must equip people to do a meaningful job of leading the people in worship. Someone leading a call to worship who has never had any experience or training in public speaking and is excessively nervous can make the whole congregation feel their discomfort. And as a result, the words proclaimed may lose their power and effectiveness.

We are often reluctant to "rehearse" the liturgies and litanies for worship. We shy away from the idea that worship is a "performance." To an extent, we do need to be mindful that it is the content that is the most important thing. However, everyone (including the readers) can worship more fully and with sincerity if there is appropriate energy, ease, and confidence in what is done. I propose that when you start to use more readers and leaders in worship, training and rehearsals should take place. This could mean simply gathering thirty minutes before the service to go over the reading or holding a day of training for all those interested in being worship leaders.

Characteristics of Different Leaders

I believe that paying attention to the energy and language of the body is essential for assigning leadership roles and developing new leaders. Here are some thoughts:

SONG LEADERS More than the ability to "conduct," song leaders are models of energy. Therefore, important factors are expressiveness in the face and body, helping us vary the dynamics in our singing, and a welcoming attitude which invites the full participation of the congregation.

LEADERS OF PRAYER Persons who have a familiarity with the congregation and exude a caring attitude will do well. These persons don't have to be good at extemporaneous prayer, but should be able to wrap whatever words are spoken in a "pastoral" presence and tone.

READERS These persons should be able to bring to the readings a variety of expressiveness that is not over-dramatic but "fits" the content. Training in projection of the voice (even in meditative reading) or microphone technique, as well as awareness of body language and posture, is recommended for these people.

LEADERS OF RITUAL ACTION These people may process items down the aisle, dress the table, or function as ushers who direct action during communion. A clear understanding by these persons of the flow of movement will help build the confidence of the congregation, especially when they are doing something "out of the ordinary." Decisive and focused gestures help us see the symbol and not the "carrier," and the comfort of the leaders of ritual will also affect the comfort level of the congregation.

THE LANGUAGE OF LEADERSHIP

As you begin to use more people in various roles as worship leaders, it is important to pay attention to the "language" of worship leadership. There are four aspects of worship leadership language that I keep in mind as I am training worship leaders.

The Language of Permission

Many of us, especially those of us who grew up in Euro-American mainline denominations, need overt permission in order to enter into a ritual that may be new to us. For instance, clapping to a song may feel too "Pentecostal" to some of us and the ritual of imposition of ashes might feel too "Catholic." Even though we may be open to integrating these experiences, it is almost a relief to hear language from leaders which acknowledges our discomfort and encourages us to see our historical connection to seemingly new things.

Language of Invitation

There are many different forms of participation. The language of invitation gives people a chance to participate in ways which feel most natural to them. When introducing a ritual action, begin statements with "I invite you to . . . " and then give an alternative, especially if the action involves interaction with others. Also, encourage people to go beyond their "comfort zones" at times in order to experience something new. The language of invitation is also important when asking people to move. This language may be well received: "I invite you to stand if you are comfortable standing," rather than "stand if you are able." I also regularly say, "if sitting is what you do best, then I invite you to sit with gusto!" To acknowledge the range of mobility in positive terms is vitally important in order to include all in the worship of God.

Language of Transition

This is one of the most important ways that worship can move from stiff didactic pieces to an inspirational spiritual experience! To be able to feel the flow of the service is an important skill for a leader of worship.

Language of Education

We cannot assume that everyone in the congregation knows the significance and meaning behind symbols and rituals used in worship. Worship leaders can bring greater understanding to these things by using the language of education. This can be done in simple ways such as saying, "As our acolytes bring the light of Christ forward, let us remember that Jesus said, 'Where two or more are gathered, there I will be also.'"

CHAPTER 5

UTILIZING *Arts* AND ARTISTS IN THE CHURCH

One of the most important things to remember about worship today is that we are only limited by our imagination as to the ways that we tell the Story. And it is vital that we tell it in a myriad of ways. The arts and artists can help us in this task. The arts help us to communicate feelings and thoughts that are sometimes difficult to express. They help us engage our own imaginations so that we are encouraged to move toward a better world— toward the commonwealth of God.

Who are the artists in your community? What could they contribute to our understanding of the Creator? It is important to become acquainted with the resources in your area. Even if you are in a small town, you could get the art or music or drama teacher from the high school involved!

There are artists in our midst! **In fact, there is an artist in each one of us**! We tend to think that if we haven't learned to write or design visuals or dance or act, then it is probably too late for us. It isn't! I hope the next pages will convince you that there are **simple yet profound ways to incorporate the arts** to a greater degree in our worship and that everyone can participate!

As always, it is important to provide education about the history of the use of arts in our religious tradition. Use some of the following "Fun Facts" about the arts in newsletters and bulletins when introducing new experiences of the arts.

FUN FACTS

Old Testament Worship

> "The festival rang with *poetry*, whether uttered on behalf of congregation or God. The words of the liturgy thus danced with rhythm and sound-play and glowed with bright images. Wedded to the poetry was *music*, the voices of many lively instruments, male and female singers, soloists and choirs, completed with congregational responses. . . . Its percussive style leads us to another sister art, *dancing*. To 'rejoice before the

Lord' meant self-evidently to dance. Led by the king and lithe specialists, the dancing of all the worshipers helped them to enter into the festal gospel and to express joy and praise. . . . The joy was the climax of the festal 'story,' the eternal event now 'done'; hence *drama* was of the very essence of the worship. . . . The poetry, music, dance and drama happened in a prepared place, the contribution of *architecture*" (Davies, p. 398).*

Drama

"The earliest evidence of rituals and drama is found in Paleolithic times. Persons related to the sacred through symbols, myths, song, dance, and mimetic activity. Scripture has examples of God's messages being dramatized: Jeremiah broke a pot to give visual force to God's threat (Jeremiah 19); Ezekiel laid on the ground to illustrate the devastation of Jerusalem (Ezekiel 4). At the Last Supper, Jesus acted out, rather than merely told his disciples, how they were to relate to others (John 13). He washed their feet" (Fink, p. 369).

Dance

"The roots of liturgical dance reach far back in time. . . . Sacred dance is found in all primitive rituals, and together with drum and chant gave expression to the fundamental religious impulses of humankind. Among both western and eastern civilizations, and on every continent . . . there is a tradition of sacred dance. . . . Dance is a primary, universal mode of religious expression, testifying to a primeval sense of the union of body and soul" (Fink, p. 314)

The Aramaic (the language Jesus spoke) word for "rejoice" is the same as the word for "dance"!

The root of the word "chorus" means "dance"!

Music

"Sound in general and music in specific have the ability not only to announce presence but to engage another in dialogue and communion. Because of sound's ability to resonate inside two individuals at the same time it has the capacity to strike a common chord and elicit sympathetic vibrations from those who hear" (Fink, p. 869).

Architecture

"Primitive Christian worship, centering in the Eucharist, was essentially domestic and so was celebrated in the private house.

*All of these quotations are taken from *The New Dictionary of Sacramental Worship*, edited by Peter E. Fink, S.J., and *The New Westminster Dictionary of Liturgy and Worship*, edited by J. G. Davies.

. . . In time, houses were bought by or given to the church and these were then specially adapted to the needs of the [church]. . . . After the victory of Constantine, with Christianity replacing the pagan cults as the state religion, worship ceased to be a family gathering and became a public occasion. Its architecture accordingly was made to correspond with civic and imperial forms. . . . Throughout the centuries, the church has had an architectural setting which has expressed the Christian understanding of worship" (Davies, p. 26).

Art

"In the first few centuries of Christian experience artists had as their focus the revelation of truths about how God acts among a beloved people. What Christ personally might have looked like had no relevance at all. . . . Artists looked to their experience and the experience of their ancestors for the definition of what God was like. Their imagery was rooted in human experience and memory" (Fink, p. 67).

WRITING LITURGY

We are all writers. Our life experience makes us experts on a relationship with God. Everyone has something to contribute. We all have stories to tell because each of our lives has significance. Some of us don't have knowledge about writing forms and composition, but this is a skill that can be learned!

The following pages are exercises to help us all write liturgy. It helps to have a form in which to organize our thoughts. There are many resources about writing and journaling. I encourage you to offer time to write together in your church's small group life. It can be a wonderful spiritual practice as well as provide fodder for worship design.

HERE ARE SOME OTHER SUGGESTIONS ABOUT WRITING

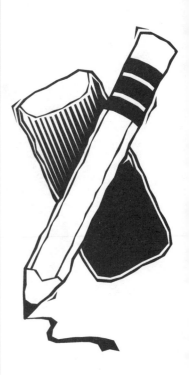

- Do some creative exercises to get into the flow and practice of writing. Here is a fun one: have everyone come up with a brainstormed list of ten words on a particular subject and then to try to use as many words on the list as possible in a paragraph or prayer.

- Have the group write "I believe . . ." statements and put them together as an affirmation of faith.

- Start a writing group that studies the lectionary or upcoming scriptures and shares their journaling with the worship team as fodder for worship.

- Have the group write several one-sentence thoughts on a particular theme or word (e.g., "gather") and then group the sentences in two's or three's.

- Put a simple sung refrain (like a global "Alleluia") between the clumps of phrases. The litany is then read by all or by several people. For example: "We gather to give thanks for this day! We gather to greet one another in Christ!" *(sing Alleluia)* "We gather to support one another in love. We gather to show our love for justice" *(sing Alleluia, etc.).*

- Ask the congregation to submit short poems or prose for a booklet and then have a poetry "coffeehouse" where these are shared and the booklets sold for a fund-raising effort.

- Get Ruth Duck's helpful guide, *Finding Words for Worship*, for excellent help with writing liturgy. *Let the Whole Church Say Amen!* by Laurence Hull Stookey is a wonderful guide for creating and delivering prayers in worship. Read Pat Schneider's book called *The Writer As an Artist: A New Approach to Writing Alone and with Others.* It has many ideas for creative writing exercises.

GOD OF MANY NAMES

Talking about God, praying to God, and proclaiming God's good news will inevitably challenge us to plunge into the depths of how to name the unnameable. And if we begin to use many names to describe God, we may find ourselves afraid of losing our grasp on who God is to us. Unfortunately, we sometimes stop the conversation too soon or focus too narrowly on one aspect of naming God (e.g., whether to use "Father" or "Mother"). I hope the following is helpful for a refreshed and constructive conversation on the myriad of ways God calls us to be the divine "image." And I hope it will help you as you try your hand at the writing exercises that follow in the next few pages.

> *Lover of Life, Wound of Compassion, Love's Tender Touch*
> *we pray earnestly for the grace*
> *to live the gift of this day unfolding*
> *in the truth and beauty*
> *of Your Life*
> *in us.*
> —*Noel Davis*

One of my favorite poets, Australian Noel Davis (*Love Finds a Way*), wrote this prayer opening. In it, he asks God to help us live the "truth and beauty" of God in us. In naming God in three evocative ways in the first line, we discover three ways that this God-in-us is to be lived out. We are to be "lovers of life," for God delights in the life of creation. We are to have "compassion" because we, as God did through Jesus, have experienced woundedness. We are to love each other through "tender touch" as God has loved us in the same way. These experiences of who God is demonstrate what I believe to be the essential reason we need diverse ways to name God:

Being faithful does not start with doing good—it starts with loving God and coming to love how God loves and whom God loves.

Well, we know who God loves—friends and enemies alike—all of creation. But knowing how to do this is not so easy. We can only continually learn the myriad of ways that God loves so that we might live our lives faithfully. We do this in describing the experience of how God has loved us. The Bible is rich with names for God (hundreds!) that describe God's action and love. For example:

as one who keeps promises	"Covenant of the People"	Isaiah 42:6
as one who dispenses grace	"Gracious God"	Jonah 4:2
as one who gives light	"Great Light"	Isaiah 9:2
as one who gives energy	"Quickening Spirit"	1 Corinthians 15:45
as one who gives shelter	"A Refuge"	Psalm 9:9
as one who brings forth life	"Seed"	Isaiah 65:9
as one who refreshes	"Well of Living Water"	Song of Solomon 4:15

EXERCISE: How have you experienced God's love? I remember a time in my life when I felt God picked me up out of the depths of sorrow. And so a prayer which begins "Holy Comforter" or "One Who Lifts Us Up" will describe one understanding of who God is for me. And God will be "incarnate" in the world when I, too, comfort others in their sorrow. Repeat this exercise with your group. Discover the many names that help us praise our God more deeply and live our lives more faithfully.

1. EXPERIENCE OF GOD'S LOVE:

_____

2. NAME TO DESCRIBE GOD:

_____

3. HOW WE ARE CALLED TO LOVE IN RESPONSE:

_____

EXERCISE!

COME, HOLY SPIRIT: WRITING A LITURGICAL POEM

Come, Holy Spirit!
Like a wind *you rush through me.*

} *Identify a metaphor,*
"Like a _____"

    Through you I am alive.
I am awakened with the knowledge that, by you,
      I am created,
         I am born,
            I have breath.

} *Descriptor #1,*
"Through you, I _____"
(then tell about it . . .)

Through you, I am present.
Spirit, you give life to this form which is me,
    and I make my unique impression in this world.
Even when all is still,
    you make your presence known.

} *Descriptor #2,*
"Through you, I _____"
(then tell about it . . .)

Spirit Wind, through you I have joy.
    I am filled with the wonder
    of my movements on this earth—
        this life improvisation.
I delight in that which I create, through you.

} *Descriptor #3,*
"Through you, I _____"
(then tell about it . . .)

Through you I have strength.
You enable me to press on in the face of difficulty.
I am challenged to become even more than I could dream
    and I am aware of the importance of each small step.

} *Descriptor #4,*
"Through you, I _____"
(then tell about it . . .)

Sustain me, Creator,
Giver of life,
    strength,
      joy,
        presence.
Free me to be all that you call me to be.

List the descriptors as a final statement

Note: I wrote the prayer poem above for use with a dance for the BBC television Lenten series by the same name (Come, Holy Spirit). Because it was made for TV, we could use a fan to produce wind as I danced. Even if you don't use dance, you can add movement to a poem simply by having candles lit or processed (if fire is your metaphor) or hearing the sound of running water from a garden fountain (if your metaphor is water). Explore the possibilities!

Write your own prayer poem about the Holy Spirit!

1 Choose a main metaphor to work with (wind, flame, fire, water, etc.)

2 List several descriptors that relate to the main metaphor

3 Write a sentence for each descriptor which fleshes out your thinking

4 Repeat the descriptors at the end to close

CLUSTERING

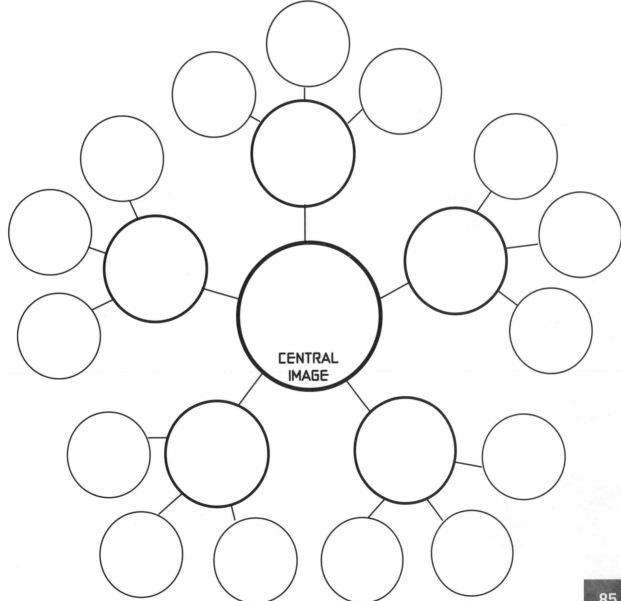

THE WORSHIP WORKSHOP

"Clustering" is a brainstorming technique that can assist in developing more vivid imagery. For instance, "comfort" is a very broad word, but phrases like "the anchor of a friend's embrace" help us to more immediately grasp the concept as lived experience.

1. Begin with an image/idea/metaphor you want to use. Write it in the central circle.

2. Place related ideas that come to mind in the next tier of clusters. As you write each idea, continue the path of that metaphor to a third tier of clusters, becoming more detailed and specific the further out you go.

3. Choose a set (or sets) of ideas that intrigue you or most fully expresses your feelings regarding the central idea. Write a prayer using as many of these chosen words as possible.

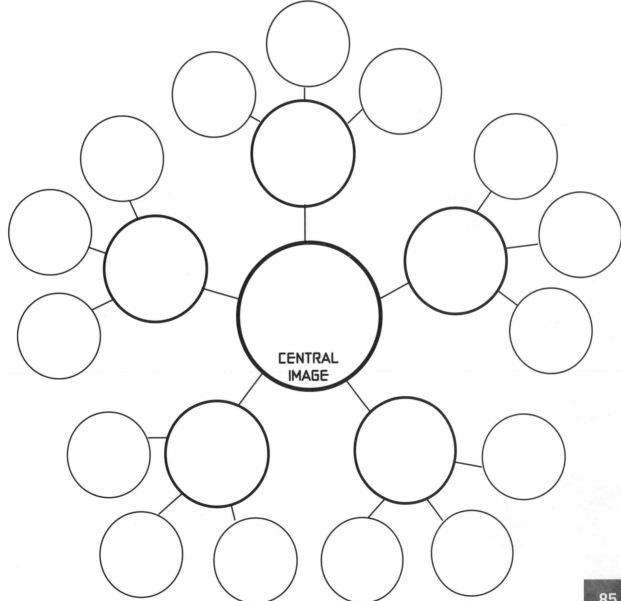

CENTRAL IMAGE

From *The Worship Workshop: Creative Ways to Design Worship Together,* by Marcia McFee. Copyright 2002 by Abingdon Press. Reproduced by permission.

TOPIC POEM/PRAYER

A topic poem/prayer uses an economy of words, but because it is concise, it can be powerfully expressive. This can be particularly useful accompanied by a graphic on a bulletin cover. This style of poem/prayer is composed of five lines:

- The first line contains only one word, a noun (though a verb would be particularly appropriate for a Call to Worship), and usually the topic of the poem/prayer.

- The second line contains two adjectives or adverbs relating to the noun or verb of the first line.

- The third line has three verbs.

- The fourth line has a four word comment.

- The fifth line is a single word that is synonymous with that used in the first line.

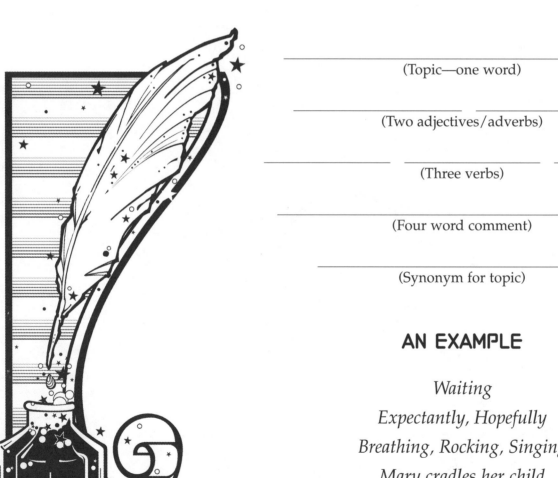

_____

(Topic—one word)

_____ _____

(Two adjectives/adverbs)

_____ _____ _____

(Three verbs)

_____

(Four word comment)

_____

(Synonym for topic)

AN EXAMPLE

Waiting

Expectantly, Hopefully

Breathing, Rocking, Singing

Mary cradles her child

Anticipation

PSALMS/HYMNS OF PRAISE

The Psalms or Hymns of Praise were the fundamental expression and hymnody of Israel's worship of God. These are God-centered in that they focus the eyes and heart of the worshiper on God, rather than on her/his own cries and problems. Some examples of hymns of praise are Psalms 8; 100; 103–105; 111; 145–150. There are three elements in the composition of this type of prayer. Using the descriptions of those elements below, compose your own hymn of praise.

I. CALL TO PRAISE

Name/describe God (God + a metaphor—"God, our keeper")

_____ ,

Praise that name and the glory of that name
   ("We praise your name and . . . ")

_____

_____ .

2. REASON FOR PRAISE

Praise God for what God is ("You are . . . ")

_____

_____ .

Praise God for what God does (God+ verb—"You cradled us . . . ")

_____

_____ .

3. RENEWED SUMMONS TO PRAISE

Reiteration of the call to praise (repeat some wording of #1)

_____ .

From *The Worship Workshop: Creative Ways to Design Worship Together*, by Marcia McFee. Copyright 2002 by Abingdon Press. Reproduced by permission.

PSALMS OF LAMENT

Nearly half of the Psalms are songs of lament and poems of complaint. "Something is deeply amiss in Israel's life with God. And Israel is not at all reluctant to voice what is troubling about its life." In voicing complaints, we are turned from denial to strong, truth-telling protest. The psalms of lament are transformative, for grief turns to praise at the end, in a show of confidence in God's grace and help. The classic model of these utterances of grief has six elements. Not all are used in every psalm. Use some or all of these elements to compose your own Psalm of Lament.

1. Name and describe God in an intimate address (e.g., "My God, God of my ancestors . . . ")

2. Tell God, with some specificity, what the trouble in life is.

3. Focus on petition. This is the point of it all. Ask God to act.

4. Add motivations. Give God some good reasons for acting.

5. Express in extremes (in other words, emphatically) the hurt.

6. End in rejoicing and praise. The mood and tone changes here. The speaker is spent and so ends by expressing confidence in God.

From *The Worship Workshop: Creative Ways to Design Worship Together,* by Marcia McFee. Copyright 2002 by Abingdon Press. Reproduced by permission.

DRAMATIZING

I use the word "dramatize" instead of "drama" to mean a much wider definition of the things we can do in worship to bring meaning to the Christian Story. One way to "dramatize" is to **embody the Word proclaimed in a more explicit form**.

BAPTISM What if a very long piece of blue cloth was extended down the center aisle or through the congregation and all the people became connected to it by touching it or holding hands with someone who is connected through other people to the cloth? The baby (if it is an infant baptism) is then wrapped in the end of the cloth closest to the front. We are reminded of our connection as the Body of Christ through our baptism and we become a living, three-dimensional symbol of our connection to the newly baptized person.	**COMMUNION** What if the style in which communion is received was dependent upon the message for the day? If we have been emphasizing the metaphor of the "family of God," it may be meaningful to receive communion around the table in smaller groupings. We may want to come forward to receive communion and kneel if we are emphasizing an offering of ourselves, but the theme of stewardship and service may be better symbolized by serving one another.

Monotony comes in many forms. Anything done the same way without variation is difficult to continue to comprehend easily. The routine format allows our minds to wander. Have you ever realized that the scripture was just read and you didn't hear a word of it? I have!

Making the reading of scripture more **dramatic**, and therefore more **communicative**, is easy and fun to do! Of course, you can get as complicated as you want in presenting drama, but it need not be. Drama can also be used in simple ways that take little preparation. It is imperative to vital worship that we not wait for a drama team to be formed and have lots of rehearsals to infuse our scriptural interpretations with drama. Take a look at these examples and then don't hesitate to create your own!

A READING FROM THE GOSPEL OF MARK

Here is an example of a narrative scripture (Mark 1:21-28) that gives the congregation a role.

> Reader: *They went to Capernaum; and when the sabbath came, he entered the synagogue and taught. They were astounded at his teaching, for he taught them as one having authority, and not as the scribes. Just then there was in their synagogue a man with an unclean spirit, and he cried out,*
> People: **"What have you to do with us, Jesus of Nazareth? Have you come to destroy us? I know who you are, the Holy One of God."**
> Reader: *But Jesus rebuked him, saying, "Be silent, and come out of him!" And the unclean spirit, convulsing him and crying with a loud voice, came out of him. They were all amazed, and they kept on asking one another,*
> People: **"What is this? A new teaching—with authority! He commands even the unclean spirits, and they obey him."**
> Reader: *At once his fame began to spread throughout the surrounding region of Galilee. This is the word of God.*
> People: **Thanks be to God!**

A PSALM READING

The psalm reading can be a wonderful Call to Worship. Adding instruments in "surround sound" can help us to understand that worship happens in the whole of the sanctuary, not just the "front and center," and it helps us feel that we are a part of this great Drama. This psalm lends itself to interpretation by the choir. I suggest that the choir space themselves around the periphery of the congregation. If you have handbells or chimes (or bells of any kind), these can be added to help with the joyful crescendo of this reading.

Psalm 126

(choir surrounding congregation; playing, singing, and bringing things to the table)

Narrator: (from the lectern or pulpit)
When the LORD restored the fortunes of Zion,
we were like those who dream. (soft ringing of a few bells)
Then our mouth was filled with laughter, (add more bells)
and our tongue with shouts of joy; (add more bells)
then it was said among the nations, (stop bell ringing)
"The LORD has done great things for them."

Choir: (emphatically)
The LORD has done great things for us,
and we rejoiced.

Narrator:
Restore our fortunes, O LORD,
[instrumental introduction starts here to joyful choir
  introit or opening hymn; the choir processes
  forward with "sheaves" (offerings of some
  kind) to place on the table]
like the watercourses in the Negeb.
May those who sow in tears
reap with shouts of joy.
Those who go out weeping,
bearing the seed for sowing,
shall come home with shouts of joy,
carrying their sheaves.

(Sing Introit and/or Opening Hymn; congregation stands)

DRAMATIZING

A CALL TO WORSHIP

Here is a Call to Worship that uses several scripture passages to introduce the theme of light in a dramatic and participatory way. This example was put together for a Pentecost service. It is appropriate to light the Paschal candle again on Pentecost, remembering the association to baptisms and also the "baptism" of the church by the Holy Spirit as represented by flames in the Acts 2 account.

A lone voice sings a cappella from the back of the sanctuary:
"*We will walk with each other, we will walk hand in hand*
We will walk with each other, we will walk hand in hand
And together we'll spread the news
that God is in our land . . ."

A narrator reads (or several readers could act as narrators); a choir begins to walk forward from the back, led by a lantern or candle:

Narrator: When the people of Israel fled from Egypt they came to the edge of the wilderness. The Lord went in front of them in a pillar of cloud by day, to lead them along the way, and in a pillar of fire by night, to give them light, so that they might travel by day and by night.

The choir sings, "Thy word is a lamp unto my feet and a light unto my path."

Narrator: David spoke to the Lord the words of this song on the day when the Lord delivered him from the hand of all his enemies. "Indeed, you are my lamp, O Lord, the Lord lightens my path."

The refrains are repeated each time, the congregation joins in, the choir continues to move forward among the people and as each reading is heard, other candles are lit.

Narrator: Isaiah, the prophet, spoke the word of God to the people of Israel, saying, "Arise, shine; for your light has come, and the glory of the Lord has risen upon you."

Refrain

Narrator: "You are the light of the world," said Jesus. "A city built on a hill cannot be hid. No one after lighting a lamp puts it under the bushel basket, but on the lampstand, and it gives light to all in the house. In the same way, let your light shine before others."

Refrain

Narrator: "I am the light of the world. Whoever follows me will never walk without light but will have the light of life."

Refrain (the Paschal candle is lit)

Narrator: We light the Christ candle today to remind us that we are the Body of Christ, empowered by the Holy Spirit to be the light of Christ in the world. As it is told in the scriptures, let us again proclaim . . .

**People: "God is light and in God there is no deception at all.
If we walk in the light as God is in the light,
we have fellowship with one another."**

The people sing "We are one in the Spirit, We are one in the Lord. . . ."

<u>Note:</u> *All of these scripture dramatizations should take one rehearsal. I have found that often it is preferable to send the script to the readers a few days before for their review and then arrange to practice in the sanctuary an hour before the service begins with the sound system and musicians (if there is music involved). Do one read-through while standing in a close-knit group to become familiar with the energy and timing between voices and then move to prescribed positions in the room. Read once from this position, make brief suggestions about vocal intonation, intensity, and volume and then read through a final time. End with a group prayer asking God to bless the reading and hearing of the scripture and thanking God for the opportunity to serve.*

<u>Note:</u> *Of course, I encourage you to consider pulling together a* **drama or biblical storytelling team** *that would prepare more complex dramas. But I believe that there are so many simple ways to bring the Story alive as well! And I have witnessed so much acceptance of and excitement about these simple forms.*

VISUALS

As I plan worship, I study scripture, consult with the preacher and musicians, and try to come up with **a central image** or idea, which embodies, or represents best, the message proclaimed. The central image will probably bring to mind several different aspects of the message, but I will want to be sure to keep focus on one major image so that it will be memorable. For example, I once helped to design services that focused on the idea of our "connection" (to God and to one another). The central image, or symbol, was a mobile. Different pieces were added at each service. When looking at the mobile as a symbol, several things came to mind besides the obvious connection among the pieces that keeps it a whole. The importance of each piece to the balance, harmony, and movement of the whole are also represented in the mobile and these ideas were also lifted up as symbols of our faith journey together. But the *central* image focused on our connection.

When introducing a fresh symbol, it is important to:

■ Make sure that the congregation is given several opportunities to connect the image to the idea. A teaser in the newsletter, a blurb in the bulletin, as well as carefully worded introductions and relevant liturgy all help us "get on board" and make it a meaningful experience.

■ Give the congregation an opportunity to interact with the symbol. If "God as our rock and our redeemer" is the theme, invite congregants to bring rocks from home or exchange small rocks as a sign of our steadfast commitment and foundation of faith. In the above "mobile" image, small groups (Sunday school or Bible study) were invited to make their own mobiles as they explored the idea of "connection."

Here are other examples:

PENTECOST! What if everyone was invited to wear red to church? Or invited to bring a red candle to be lit and placed on several tables during the service (with extras available for visitors)? What if a garden fountain (living water—it sounds great!) was used for either a baptism or remembrance of baptism? What if red fabric was hung in the sanctuary and a hidden fan softly blew them, calling to mind both flames and wind? What if red helium balloons (it is a birthday party, you know) were tied or taped to each pew or chair and the congregation took them outside at the end of the service to release and be "carried by the Spirit"?

CONFIRMATION! What if a weather balloon with the names of confirmands written on it was used as a focal point for the service and then released into the air outside? They could literally see how the Holy Spirit empowers them to go out into the world!

HANDOUT

POTTERY! (or use a real potter at the wheel!) "You are the potter, I am the clay. . . . " Use the pottery as a symbol of our being "vessels," or broken pottery to symbolize our brokenness (check out Jeremiah on this one!), or dip the fruit of the vine for communion out of a large clay pot with a ladle, focusing on the wedding at Cana.

FEET! "In His Footsteps" was a theme emphasizing discipleship and the faith journey that I used for a special series of services. We had butcher block paper rolled out on the floor of the nave and people were invited to draw an outline of their feet in magic marker and write words of hope for the journey inside. This "road" full of footsteps was used in the sanctuary then as paraments for pulpit, lectern, and table.

BOXES! A day of celebration of mission included stuffing boxes with health kits, school kits, rice, beans, and so forth. So we continued the use of boxes in the worship service through a drama in which boxes represented different social concerns such as illiteracy, disease, disaster, and hunger.

SALT! Salt was used in the biblical world as a symbol of covenant. Before refrigeration, salt was a preservative; therefore, the people exchanged salt as a sign that they would "preserve" their promise. In a service of commitment I have had congregations exchange salt pellets with one another in the same way, while learning something new about biblical history!

SIGNS OF THE TIMES! In worship at a retreat, we used road signs such as "Stop," "Yield," and "Danger" to talk about our faith journey. On the other side of the signs, which we turned around during the service were the words, "Listen," "Pray," and "Slow Down." You could probably think of many more "signs" to use!

WALLS! I worked with a church once that brought in all kinds of construction items like sawhorses, ladders, tools, and even warning barricades from construction sites. They focused for three weeks on "tearing down the walls" (not literally!) we have built within us, and between us that separate us from God.

<u>*Note:*</u> *I recommend creating visuals around a series of services rather than something different every week. This can become time consuming and having something different every week can become as monotonous as having the same thing every week. Also, a balance of very ordinary objects and time-honored symbols is important.*

BULLETIN COVERS!

Some recommendations about bulletins (or "worship guides"):

■ Use a **larger format** to give yourselves room to include new music and graphics. An 11″x17″ folded sheet of paper with an insert for announcements and prayer lists works well. People can then take the insert home and put in on the refrigerator. Consider using a graphic and scripture quotation to remind worshipers of the service throughout the week.

■ Use **graphics that help communicate the message or theme for the day** rather than a drawing or picture of the church on the bulletin front. People already know what the church looks like— they just came in!

Here are some examples:

USE A GRAPHIC ON THE FRONT AND EVEN START THE ORDER OF SERVICE AROUND IT!

Wednesday
Communion Service
Clergy Retreat
October 13, 1999

Call to Worship
Leviticus 25:9-10

One: We have come proclaiming
    Jubilee!

**All: We have gathered to renew,
release, reconcile, and rejoice.**

One: Renewing of mind, body, and
    spirit. Releasing the captive within
    us, Reconciling the alienated,
    Rejoicing in God's great mercy.

**All: The day of atonement has
come! The trumpet sounds.
Let the Jubliee begin!**

Sung Response:
"Blow Ye the Trumpet, Blow"
    vv 1, 2, & 6 UMH #379

Other ideas:

■ Use pictures of the congregation at work in mission or in fellowship. Digital cameras make this so easy!

■ Use photographs of scenery. There are many electronic collections of photos that can be used royalty-free!

■ Have the congregation give input about the theme ahead of time and use their comments on the covers throughout the season.

■ Ask the children to draw pictures of biblical stories to copy and use as covers.

BULLETIN COVERS! (CONTINUED)

COMMISSION AN ARTIST TO DRAW SOME COVERS FOR YOU! THIS ONE IS BY ALICIA WHITE DAILY.

USE AN ABSTRACT SHAPE AS THE BASIS FOR COVERS.

Lake Junaluska
Thursday, July 16, 1998
The Morning Word of Grace

Balance

Preparation for the Service
Music for Gathering

A Time of Centering

An ancient saying:
"When I look at your heavens,
the work of your fingers,
the moon and the stars
that you have established;
what are human beings that you are
mindful of them, mortals that you care
for them?"
Psalm 8:3-4

A contemporary saying:
"Imagination is more imporant
than knowledge."
Albert Einstein

Just as you may design a worship center for an entire season, also use distinct designs for the worship guide for an entire liturgical season rather than changing every Sunday (or never changing!). As you can see, I like the term "worship guide" rather than "bulletin." It helps us understand the function of this device as well as suggesting that the worship is what we do, not simply what we read!

USE VARIOUS QUOTATIONS ON THE COVER.

CELEBRATE THE "ART" OF SUMMER!

Summer is a time when many people take off for vacations, work camps, summer camps, or trips to visit relatives. As worship leaders, we lament that the pews may not be full in the summer, but we celebrate that people can take the opportunity to enjoy more of God's creation! How can we invite people to feel a part of their church community even when they are away? And how can we learn more about each other, sharing our experiences and thoughts, once we have returned?

Vacations, camps, and mission trips help us to step back from the "everyday" of our lives and reflect from a different environment and perspective.

What if members were encouraged to write their reflections in the form of prayers, poems, or prose to be compiled into a church-wide collection? Advent devotional booklets are such a hit we needn't limit our offerings to this one-time-a-year endeavor. One church where I worked **compiled a book of poetry and prose and then held a "coffeehouse" poetry reading** complete with cappuccino, sweets, and a fellowship hall transformed with little white lights and tables covered with beautiful cloths and candles!

With camera technology these days, everyone is a good photographer! What if members were invited to select a photo from their summer escapades, frame it, and exhibit it at a church-wide **photo and art exhibit** called "In Celebration of Creation!"

97

MOVEMENT

Movement is

an everyday language—we use gestures to communicate all the time!

an inherent (first) language—movement came before words!

a universal language—we often revert to "hand signals" when we don't know the language!

an interpretive language—to add movement is to become a living three-dimensional symbol!

Dance has been a part of our religious heritage in many different time periods. Using movement to interpret and express our faith experiences is an important part of praising God with "every ounce of our being."

Because I have a background in professional dance, I have several resources that you may find helpful if you would like to explore using dance in worship. *Creating a Dance for Worship* is a resource that helps dancers who have movement skills but have never choreographed for a worship service. *Four Prayers for the Morning* is a videotape that uses simple stretching accompanied by music and scripture as a form of devotion. There are also other books about sacred dance listed in the Resource Listing.

But "interpretive movement" does not have to be limited to movement by people we call "dancers"! Here are several other ways to use movement in worship:

■ Have the congregation face the center of the sanctuary to sing a round so that we experience being in a kind of circle.

■ Have the congregation face each other across the aisle for a call and response litany or a creed.

■ Invite the congregation to come forward and dip their hands in the water of a fountain or bowl to remember their baptism.

■ Assume different "prayer postures" like hands clenched, clasped, or open, or placing their heads in their hands (as you will see in the Prayer of Confession on page 101).

■ Invite the congregation to use washable markers to make the sign of the fish on each other's hands, recalling the early Christian community's practice of making this identifying sign. The children and youth could facilitate this.

■ Try simple clapping, swaying, or stepping from side to side with an appropriate global song. See Michael Hahn's *Halle, Halle: We Sing the World 'Round* for ideas. Don't forget that leaders and choir must model this for the congregation.

So do you see how "movement" can be used in simple ways as well as complex dances? Introducing the use of movement should include educating everyone about the biblical and historical use of dance in worship. It is often good to use movement in a simple way at first, like processing fabric and "dressing the table" or having some young people do an Israeli candle dance at a special night time service.

The following pages include some examples for your use. The movements to the Lord's Prayer are often a hit, especially when introduced by children or young people and the Prayer of Confession and Assurance is a good start to a different "prayer posture." The following page about movement includes some tips about using interpretive movement in the form of "do's and don'ts."

"DO'S AND DON'TS" ABOUT LITURGICAL MOVEMENT

After twenty-five years of dancing in church, I definitely have some opinions about it. And so, unabashedly, here they are:

DO introduce dance to a congregation with education and preparation. An understanding of the historical, biblical, and theological foundations will do wonders for a congregation's ability to worship through this ancient form.

DO NOT invite dancers to just come and do a "special number."

DO make sure that dance is used within the context of the liturgy and is grounded theologically in the focus of the service.

DO encourage people who have had little to no dance training to participate in drama and symbolic movement.

DO NOT, however, let them stand on one leg or try a double pirouette. They will be uncomfortable and I guarantee the congregation will be also! Simple is often the most poignant.

DO NOT wear leotards and tights (this is not a widely held opinion).

DO dress like a real human being (in clothes that allow you to move freely) when interpreting the lives and feelings of human beings rather than dressing like an otherworldly creature. People in the pews will more readily relate to you if they aren't terrified of imagining themselves in your shoes.

DO wear clothes that enhance, rather than detract from, the message. Meaningful and appropriate color and texture are important features.

DO allow creative and diverse and sometimes even abstract expressions of dance.

DO NOT expect a dancer to symbolize every word of an anthem or scripture. If that is what you want, find a sign language interpreter instead.

DO NOT simply tell people what they are going to do. Rather, develop a language of invitation and choice when encouraging the congregation to experience movement together.

DO have leaders who are initiating and modeling the movement confidently.

DO understand "liturgical movement" for what it literally means— "liturgy, the work of the people." Movement is a common language, a first language, for all people. While there are diverse abilities, there is always an important place for the divine language of life itself. Liturgical movement is not just something trained dancers do. It can be as simple as the people moving to receive communion or facing one another during the reciting of a creed. The focus of the "work of the people" where movement is concerned should be on this question: "How can we embody the Word of God proclaimed?"

99

THE LORD'S PRAYER

It may be helpful to teach this prayer (an adaptation of Michael Mansfield's Lord's Prayer in gestures) to the children during a time when they come forward and then have the children repeat it as they "teach" the adults. This seems to encourage the participation of those who are hesitant about trying something new (children and adults alike!).

Start by inviting everyone to find a partner and stand facing them. Tell them that if there is no one free around them, they can join in with another pair to make a threesome. The prayer will work fine with three.

It may work best to teach the movements first without telling anyone even what words will be used to accompany them. Then, add the words, yet continue to give verbal cues for the movement. Then, you are ready to do it again (adding the adults) so that everyone can experience it in a prayerful (yet joyful) manner. The following is a description of the movements that accompany the words. The descriptions occur simultaneously with the words, which precede them on the page.

"Our Father . . . (or other name for God)"
> (start with the arms bent in front of you, palms facing up)

"who art in Heaven . . . "
> (place the hands on the chest over the heart)

"hallowed be thy name . . . "
> (extend the arms in an upward diagonal direction, meeting your partner's hands high—like London Bridge)

"Thy kingdom come . . . "
> (look up to one set of hands and reach up further, separating them)

"Thy will be done . . . "
> (bring those hands and arms down to your sides)

"on earth . . . "
> (look up to the other set of hands and reach up further, separating them)

"as it is in heaven."
> (bring those hands and arms down to your sides)

"Give us this day our daily bread . . . "
> (cup your two hands together in front of you as if receiving something)

"and forgive us our trespasses . . . "
> (make a fist and press your knuckles against your partner's knuckles)

"as we forgive those who trespass against us . . . "
> (unclench your fists and link fingers, holding hands with your partner in front of you)

"And lead us not into temptation . . . "
> (continue to hold hands, turn them upside-down to reveal wrists)

"but deliver us from evil . . . "
> (let go of hands in a releasing, freeing quality, arms end open to sides)

"For thine is the kingdom . . . "
> (shake right hands as in a hand shake and don't let go)

"and the power . . . "
> (shake left hands as in a hand shake; now you have both hands clasped)

"and the glory forever . . . "
> (give your clasped hands a rousing shake on "glory"—this gets smiles!)

"Amen."
> (let go of hands)

Movements set to a familiar prayer such as this can give us some fresh "food for thought." They become three-dimensional, spatial theological statements (which is reason to give great care to "interpretive movement"). What does the experience of being "knuckle-to-knuckle" tell us about "trespasses"? And what analogies can be drawn between forgiveness and the opening of fists to link fingers? How do exposed wrists speak to us of the vulnerability of "temptation"? And how is "the kingdom and the power" of God like holding hands with a neighbor? Enjoy!

PRAYER OF CONFESSION AND SIGNS OF ASSURANCE

Introduction

Note: Print only the response in bold at the end of the prayer in your worship guide.

Leader: The forehead is a place of connection. It is a place of caring. We go there to check for a fever, to sooth worry lines, to comfort. We cradle our head in our hands when we feel stressed; we massage our temples when we feel pain. And it is where, for me as an infant, the minister of the church placed his/her wet hand and baptized me in the love and power of the divine Three in One. It is a place of connection. And so, I invite you to place your head in your hands as a posture for our prayer of confession this morning. Let us pray.

Prayer

OH, GOD . . . WE FORGET.
How quickly we forget the touch of our baptism, the connection to our call. A wet hand to our forehead, cleansing, anointing us—connecting us as members of the Body of Christ. We are so often hesitant to respond.

WE FORGET.
We forget the touch of a cool hand to our hot foreheads. We are reluctant to reach out to touch the blazing fever that rages among your people. We are afraid, so we retreat, prescribing instead of soothing, looking and not touching, unconnected.

WE FORGET.
We forget what it is like to reflect truthfully about ourselves. We are unwilling to sit with ourselves, holding our head in our hands, hesitant to claim your possibilities for us, reluctant to name our sin.

Be with us as a parent who sits with a child. Patiently, painfully, wrapping us in your love and care—even when we refuse to be touched. Send us your merciful healing. We ask for your grace and peace, that by it, we might have the courage to stay connected. Amen.

Signs of Assurance

The good news, friends, is that the forgiveness, grace, and peace of Jesus Christ is with us. I invite you to turn to your neighbor or neighbors and exchange names. And, as a sign of assurance and with their permission, place your hand on their forehead, their shoulder, or simply their hand—connected in some way—and speak these words of blessing and assurance to one another:

"You are a child of God! Blessed are you!"

Note: An alternative to the prayer posture is to have a parent and child in a rocking chair. Instead of inviting people to rest their head in their hands, the introduction to the prayer would conclude with "I invite you to gaze upon this image of mother/father and child to aid us in praying this morning." I often ask the pianist to play "Jesus Loves Me" softly during the prayer.

MUSIC

There are so many incredible resources for music. Other resources can tell you much more about the technique and intricacies of sacred music. But I do have some things to say about music. (Not a surprise, right?)

First, what is "sacred" music? My values about music are very much the same as my ideas about all the other media used in worship. Music needs to have theological depth and stylistic diversity, and it must serve to communicate the message, help us praise God and pray to God, and help us on our spiritual journey. These are the "ground rules," and within them we need all the other characteristics we talked about at the beginning of this workbook: **interactive, intergenerational, interesting, and inspiring!**

To this end, I believe that we must take music out of the "music box" (so to speak) and use our imaginative tools. Here are some various ways to use music.

PERCUSSION—It has historical roots and can help us center and listen in a different way. I especially use African drums or hand drums and rainsticks to accompany processions, readings, and introits ("Come into God's Presence Singing Alleluia!") and sung prayers ("Spirit of the Living God").

SOLO INSTRUMENTS—I like to have a solo instrument like a violin or saxophone play a melody to transition us through the service. Then the melody comes alive in the closing hymn.

SURROUND SOUND—One of my favorite ways to give the call to worship is to have instrumentalists surrounding the congregation. The sounds can be interspersed with a psalm or poem. This idea works well with a bell choir and random ringing.

"MUSICAL PUNCTUATION"—This term was coined by my good friends Jane Marshall and John Thornburg who have written many such "punctuations." Musical Punctuations are short congregational refrains that lead us into or out of a part of the liturgy. My favorite comes before a scripture and says, "Because the words we wait to hear could shake us to the core, be with us Lord!" Taizé refrains are great to use, especially to punctuate prayer.

INTERSPERSED WITH READINGS—Most hymnals have a scripture index in the back. Check it frequently to see if there is a hymn about a chosen text that could be sung interspersed with the scripture reading. You could also write prayers that would complement verses of a hymn. This combination helps us listen and comprehend both the text of the reading and the hymn better.

USING NEW WORDS WITH FAMILIAR TUNES—If some in the congregation are resistant to "new music" at first, composers have wonderful new texts that can fit with familiar tunes. Using this concept, we can broaden our vocabulary of praise! If you like the words of a hymn but the tune is difficult, look at the metrical index in the back of the hymn book and find a more familiar tune to sing with the new words.

MUSIC

(CONTINUED)

Here are some more examples of using music in diverse ways:

USING A HYMN AS PART OF PRAYER

Use the following verses of "Open My Eyes, That I May See" by Clara H. Scott to enhance a time of prayer.

Preparation for Prayer

Open my eyes, that I may see glimpses of truth thou hast for me;
place in my hands the wonderful key that shall unclasp and set me free.
Silently now I wait for thee,
ready, my God, thy will to see.
Open my eyes, illumine me,
Spirit divine!

A Time of Silent Prayer

Open my ears, that I may hear voices of truth thou sendest clear;
and while the wavenotes fall on my ear, everything false will disappear.
Silently now I wait for thee,
ready, my God, thy will to see.
Open my ears, illumine me,
Spirit divine!

Pastoral Prayer

(please send children forward during this verse)
Open my mouth, and let me bear gladly the warm truth everywhere;
open my heart and let me prepare love with thy children thus to share.
Silently now I wait for thee,
ready, my God, thy will to see.
Open my heart, illumine me,
Spirit divine!

The Lord's Prayer (led by the children)

USING DIVERSE INSTRUMENTATION

- What if the children of the church made simple rhythm instruments during the month of May for use in the Pentecost service by *everyone* to make a "joyful noise" during a rousing rendition of "I'm Gonna Sing When the Spirit Says Sing"? What if people came in and these instruments were already in the pews?

- What if wind chimes were placed at several hidden spots in the sanctuary and sounded at several surprising times during the service to symbolize the Holy Spirit moving mysteriously among us? This musical cue brings special attention to whatever is being said at the time of the chime.

From *The Worship Workshop: Creative Ways to Design Worship Together*, by Marcia McFee. Copyright 2002 by Abingdon Press. Reproduced by permission.

MUSIC

INTRODUCING PARTS OF THE LITURGY WITH FAMILIAR REFRAINS

"Silently now, I wait for thee . . . " (silent prayer); "Beautiful words, wonderful words, wonderful words of life . . . " (scripture reading); "Thy Word is a lamp unto my feet . . . " (procession of the light of Christ and the Bible); "Come, thou long expected Jesus, born to set thy people free . . . " (Confession and Assurance). A fun thing to do is go through the hymnal looking for refrains to use in this way!

INTERSPERSING A LITANY AND A HYMN

To highlight Ecumenical Sunday, try interspersing the verses of the hymn, "We Utter Our Cry" with spoken words by the congregation. If you have multimedia capabilities, show pictures that correspond to the verses of the hymn with the words overlaid. Use these or write your own:

(Instrumental introduction to the hymn begins)
People: With one voice, we utter our cry to you. We unite with all those who, in prayer and mission engage with those who suffer. *Verse 1*

People: We unite with all those who confront violence and work for peace in our neighborhoods and our world. *Verse 2*

People: We unite with all those who tend the earth and hold dear all living things. *Verse 3*

People: We unite with all those who support and engage in the process of peace. *Verse 4*

People: We unite with all those whose actions testify to God's victory over evil and who struggle for justice. *Verse 5*

People: Spirit of promise, Spirit of unity, renew in all of us the passionate desire for the coming of your kingdom. *Verse 6*

INTERSPERSING A HYMN AND SCRIPTURE

"Lord, You Have Come to the Lakeshore" *(the soloists are in three different places and are "gathered" one by one)* and Mark 1:14-20 (NIV)

Narrator: After John was put in prison, Jesus went into Galilee, proclaiming the good news of God. "The time has come," he said. "The kingdom of God is near. Repent and believe the good news!"
(Soloist #1 sings verse 1; people join in on chorus; the narrator ["Jesus"] greets soloist #1 with a hug.)

Narrator: As Jesus walked beside the Sea of Galilee, he saw Simon and his brother Andrew casting a net into the lake, for they were fishermen. "Come, follow me," Jesus said, "and I will make you fishers of [people]." At once they left their nets and followed him.
(Soloist #2 sings verse 2; people come in on chorus; narrator and soloist #1 greet #2.)

Narrator: When he had gone a little farther, he saw James son of Zebedee and his brother John in a boat, preparing their nets. Without delay he called them, and they left their father Zebedee in the boat with the hired men and followed him.
(Soloist #3 sings verse 3; people join in on chorus; all characters greet soloist #3 and exit while congregation is singing the chorus. The sermon is preached and the congregation responds afterwards by singing verse 4 and chorus.)

From *The Worship Workshop: Creative Ways to Design Worship Together,* by Marcia McFee. Copyright 2002 by Abingdon Press. Reproduced by permission.

MUSIC

My Favorite Music Resources

Here is a short list of my favorite resources and what I think you could start with in expanding your musical library.

Denominational hymnal

Take time to go through your hymnal and search for songs that may be overlooked because they are new. Many newer hymnals have a great variety of time-honored hymnody as well as gospel, global, and meditative music.

Songs and Prayers of Taizé: The People's Edition

This is a must-have! The refrains are beautiful and easy to learn. There are many editions and collections from the community in Taizé but I recommend you start with this one. This is published by GIA Publishers.

Global Praise 1 and 2

These little collections of global songs by composers all over the world was put together by the General Board of Global Ministries of the United Methodist Church as a result of several meetings of these composers. You can also order a recording to help the choir learn the songs (which will help the congregation!).

Sent by the Lord

This is another collection of global music (do you get the hint yet? *Use global music!*). It is put together by the Iona Community and published by GIA.

Common Ground: Songs for All the Churches

This collection edited by John Bell and handled in the U.S. by GIA Publishing has some wonderful new songs (including my favorite, "All Are Welcome," as well as global music, Taizé refrains, and familiar hymns).

Renew: Songs and Hymns for Blended Worship

This collection is published by Hope Publishing Company and is divided into music for the different parts of the liturgy (Gathering, Proclaiming, Responding, Sending Forth). It is a good place to see how several styles of music can be blended into the same service.

Book of Worship

There are wonderful resources for refrains and musical responses from supplementary resources to hymnals and books of worship. We often look to these for prayers and words, but also try searching them for music.

The Faith We Sing

This is a wonderful compilation put out by the United Methodist Church but intended for ecumenical use. It has an incredibly wide range of styles, traditional and new compositions, and service music. In fact, I would start here as a first addition to your collection. It includes many of my favorites from the above-mentioned resources.

Well, those are my favorites, the ones I carry around with me as my "working library" of music to design with. Don't forget: You need a license to reprint words and/or music in worship guides or project on a screen. Here are some important licenses to have: GIA (1-800-442-1358), as well as CCLI (www.ccli.com) and/or LincenSing (1-800-328-0200).

IDEAS FOR INVITING ARTISTS TO YOUR CHURCH

Visual Art

■ Create a gallery out of a hallway, entranceway, nave, vestibule, sanctuary, or fellowship hall. Invite several artists to show their work based on a certain theme ("God's People: Portraits" or "And It Was Good: Still Life").

■ Hold an opening reception after worship.

■ Hold discussions with the artist(s) during the Sunday school hour or at a special time. Ask the artists about their creative process, inspiration, and how their spirituality interacts with their artistry.

■ Incorporate a piece (or pieces) of art into worship through a sermon or children's time, or as an inspiration for prayer.

■ Invite an expert to do an educational or historical slide show "in-house," or take a trip to the local museum to view the religious art on exhibit there. This is a wonderful complement to Bible study.

Have a folk art fair. Invite several artists to show their work, giving people an idea of the range of visual art and its role in religion. Include art forms such as:
■ weaving
■ stained glass making
■ glass cutting
■ pottery
■ candle making
■ international exhibit of art from different countries and cultures

Music

JAZZ VESPERS: Celebrate spirituality through the idiom of jazz, either in a worship setting or special evening event.

DRUMMING: Use drummers and rhythm traditions from around the world to emphasize this common bond between many cultures.

HYMNODY: Lead a study on the history and theology of hymns or use hymns to enhance a Bible study. Listening to and singing music from different time periods and cultures can help us learn about the history of worship and the church.

IDEAS FOR INVITING ARTISTS TO YOUR CHURCH (CONTINUED)

CONTEMPORARY, GOSPEL, OR FOLK SINGERS: Invite local groups to participate in worship or special events.

Drama

Sponsor a theater group or youth choir that is touring. Collaborate with several churches in order to share the expenses.

Use or create a drama dealing with issues which concern the church (missions, racism, violence, etc.) and then hold a discussion forum after the production.

Film

Lead a small group in watching a series of films together and then engage in discussion related to the spirituality or theology represented in the film. This is a good way to bring meaningful exchanges to our movie-going culture!

Poetry / Prose

Sponsor a poetry reading ("coffeehouse" style) and invite persons in the congregation to share their favorite poetry.

Invite someone to come in and teach a creative writing workshop. Ask participants to contribute to a worship service. Or hold a workshop on journaling as a process of spiritual reflection.

Lead a small group series on the writings of an author who speaks to spirituality through fiction.

Dance

Invite a liturgical dancer to participate in a worship service.

Sponsor a workshop on creative movement, movement as prayer, and the history of dance in religion.

Have a "global gathering" featuring the songs and dances of diverse cultures.

107

RESOURCES, RESOURCES, RESOURCES

Since there are so many worship resources, providing a comprehensive list is not possible—nor would you want to wade through it. So, the following bibliography is a compilation of things that have been helpful to me and to the churches I've worked with. They are not denomination-specific (consult your denomination's worship area for more resources particular to your tradition). Some are practical in nature and some are books used by many seminarians but are not so highly academic that you need a Ph.D. to decipher them. Of course, if you'd like an even more scholarly approach, many of these resources have bibliographies that will point you in that direction. Finally, I list more of my favorite music resources for worship to supplement what I have already recommended on page 105. Enjoy!

Theology of Worship

Driver, Tom F. *Liberating Rites: Understanding the Transformative Power of Ritual.* Boulder, Col.: Westview Press, 1997.

Elkins, Heather Murray. *Worshiping Women: Re-forming God's People for Praise.* Nashville: Abingdon Press, 1994.

Lathrop, Gordon W. *Holy Things: A Liturgical Theology.* Minneapolis: Fortress Press, 1993.

McElvaney, William K. *Eating and Drinking at the Welcome Table: The Holy Supper for All People.* St. Louis: Chalice Press, 1998.

Moeller, Pamela Ann. *Exploring Worship Anew: Dreams and Visions.* St. Louis: Chalice Press, 1998.

Proctor-Smith, Marjorie. *In Her Own Rite: Constructing Feminist Liturgical Tradition.* Nashville: Abingdon Press, 1990.

Saliers, Don E. *Worship and Spirituality.* 2nd ed. Akron: OSL Publications, 1999.

———. *Worship as Theology: Foretaste of Glory Divine.* Nashville: Abingdon Press, 1994.

———. *Worship Come to Its Senses.* Nashville: Abingdon Press, 1996.

Walton, Janet R. *Feminist Liturgy: A Matter of Justice.* Collegeville, Minn.: Liturgical Press, 2000.

White, James F. *The Sacraments in Protestant Practice and Faith.* Nashville: Abingdon Press, 1999.

History of Worship

Berger, Teresa. *Women's Ways of Worship: Gender Analysis and Liturgical History.* Collegeville, Minn.: Liturgical Press, 1999.

Bradshaw, Paul F. and Lawrence A. Hoffman, eds. *The Making of Jewish and Christian Worship.* Notre Dame: University of Notre Dame Press, 1991.

Costen, Melva Wilson. *African American Christian Worship.* Nashville: Abingdon Press, 1993.

Hickman, Hoyt L., Don E. Saliers, Laurence Hull Stookey, and James F. White. *The New Handbook of the Christian Year.* Nashville: Abingdon Press, 1992.

White, James F. *A Brief History of Christian Worship*. Nashville: Abingdon Press, 1993.
———. *Introduction to Christian Worship*. Nashville: Abingdon Press, 1980.
———. *Protestant Worship: Traditions in Transition*. Louisville, Ky.: Westminster/John Knox Press, 1989.

Worship and the Arts

Adams, Doug. *Congregational Dancing in Christian Worship*. Austin: The Sharing Company, 1980.
———. *Eyes to See Wholeness: Visual Arts Informing Biblical and Theological Studies in Education and Worship Through the Church Year*. Prescott: Educational Ministries, 1995.
Adams, Doug and Diane Apostolos-Cappadona, eds. *Dance as Religious Studies*. New York: Crossroad Publishing, 1990.
Adams, Doug and Michael Moynahan, eds. *Postmodern Worship and the Arts*. Berkeley: Center for the Arts, Religion, and Education, 2001.
Apostolos-Cappadona, Diane, ed. *Art, Creativity, and the Sacred: An Anthology in Religion and Art*. New York: Crossroad Publishing, 1984.
De Sola, Carla. *Movement Meditations to the Songs from Taizé*. Mahway, N.J.: Paulist Press, 1996. Videocassette.
———. *The Spirit Moves: Handbook of Dance and Prayer*. Austin: The Sharing Company, 1986.
Gagne, Ronald, Thomas Kane, and Robert ver Eecke. *Introducing Dance in Christian Worship*. Washington D.C.: Pastoral Press, 1984.
Lovelace, Austin C. *Hymn Notes for Church Bulletins*. Chicago: GIA Publications, 1987.
McFee, Marcia. *Creating a Dance for Worship*. Alameda, Calif.: Peace by Peace Productions, 1995.
———. *Kinetic Meditations: Four Prayers for the Morning*. Alameda, Calif.: Peace by Peace Productions, 1998. Videocassette.
Miles, Margaret R. *Seeing and Believing: Religion and Values in the Movies*. Boston: Beacon Press, 1996.
Reynolds, William J. and Milburn Price. *A Survey of Christian Hymnody*. Carol Stream, Ill.: Hope Publishing, 1987.
Sill, Gertrude Grace. *A Handbook of Symbols in Christian Art*. New York: Macmillan, 1975.
Spencer, Donald A. *Hymn and Scripture Selection Guide: A Cross-Reference Tool for Worship Leaders*. Grand Rapids: Baker Book House, 1993.
Sydnor, James Rawlings. *Hymns and Their Uses*. Carol Stream, Ill.: Hope Publishing, 1982.
———. *Introducing a New Hymnal: How to Improve Congregational Singing*. Chicago: GIA Publications, 1989.
Wilson-Dickson, Andrew. *The Story of Christian Music: From Gregorian Chant to Black Gospel*. Minneapolis: Fortress Press, 1996.
Wilson-Kastner, Patricia. *Sacred Drama*. Minneapolis: Fortress Publishing, 1999.
Wren, Brian. *Praying Twice: The Music and Words of Congregational Song*. Louisville, Ky.: Westminster John Knox Press, 2000.
Young, Carlton R. *My Great Redeemer's Praise: An Introduction to Christian Hymns*. Akron: OSL Publications, 1995.

The Language of Worship

Duck, Ruth C. *Finding Words for Worship: A Guide for Leaders.* Louisville, Ky.: Westminster/John Knox Press, 1995.

Ramshaw, Gail. *God Beyond Gender: Feminist Christian God-Language.* Minneapolis: Fortress Press, 1995.

———. *Reviving Sacred Speech: The Meaning of Liturgical Language.* Akron: OSL Publications, 2000.

Stookey, Laurence Hull. *Let the Whole Church Say Amen! A Guide for Those Who Pray in Public.* Nashville: Abingdon Press, 2001.

Wren, Brian A. *What Language Shall I Borrow?: God-Talk in Worship: A Male Response to Feminist Theology.* New York: Crossroad Publishing, 1989.

Styles and Planning of Worship

Benedict, Daniel and Craig Kennet Miller. *Contemporary Worship for the 21st Century.* Nashville: Discipleship Resources, 1994.

Black, Kathy. *Worship Across Cultures: A Handbook.* Nashville: Abingdon Press, 1998.

Doran, Carol and Thomas H. Troeger. *Trouble at the Table: Gathering the Tribes for Worship.* Nashville: Abingdon Press, 1992.

Hickman, Hoyt L., Don E. Saliers, Laurence Hull Stookey, and James F. White. *The New Handbook of the Christian Year.* Nashville: Abingdon Press, 1992.

Sample, Tex. *The Spectacle of Worship in a Wired World.* Nashville: Abingdon Press, 1998.

Schattauer, Thomas, Karen Ward, and Mark Bangert. *What Does "Multicultural" Worship Look Like?* Minneapolis: Augsburg Fortress Press, 1996.

Webber, Robert E. *Planning Blended Worship: The Creative Mixture of Old and New.* Nashville: Abingdon Press, 1998.

Wright, Tim and Jan Wright, eds. *Contemporary Worship.* Nashville: Abingdon Press, 1997.

More Music Favorites

Batastini, Robert J., general ed. *Gather.* Chicago: GIA Publications, 1998.

Bell, John L., ed. *Common Ground: A Song Book for All the Churches.* Edinburgh: Saint Andrew Press, 1998.

Bell, John L. and Graham Maule, eds. *Come All You People: Shorter Songs for Worship.* Chicago: GIA Publications, 1994.

———. *Love & Anger: Songs of Lively Faith and Social Justice.* Chicago: GIA Publications, 1998.

Berthier, Jacques. *Music from Taizé.* Vol. 1. Chicago: GIA Publications, 1978, 1982.

———. *Songs & Prayers from Taizé.* Chicago: GIA Publications, 1991.

Boyer, Horace Clarence, ed. *Lift Every Voice and Sing II: An African American Hymnal.* New York: The Church Hymnal Corporation, 1993.

Churches in Solidarity with Women: Ecumenical Decade, 1988–1998 Prayers & Poems, Songs & Stories. 1988.

Cleveland, J. Jefferson and Virginia Nix, eds. *Songs of Zion.* Nashville: Abingdon Press, 1981.

Duck, Ruth C. *Circles of Care: Hymns and Songs.* Cleveland: Pilgrim Press, 1998.

Duck, Ruth C. and Michael G. Bausch, eds. *Everflowing Streams: Songs for Worship.* New York: Pilgrim Press, 1981.

Harling, Per. *Worshipping Ecumenically: Orders of Service from Global Meetings with Suggestions for Local Use.* Geneva: WCC Publications, 1995.

Hawn, C. Michael, ed. *For the Living of These Days: Resources for Enriching Worship.* Macon, Ga.: Smyth & Helloes Publishing, 1995.

Heafield, Susan and Brian Wren. *We Can Be Messengers: Worship Songs: Christmas, Before and After.* Decatur: Praise Partners Publishing, 2000.

Hintze, Otto and Carlos Puig, eds. ¡Cantad al Senor! St. Louis: Concordia, 1991.

Hofstra, Marilyn M., ed. *Voices: Native American Hymns and Worship Resources.* Nashville: Discipleship Resources, 1992.

Holbert, John, S T Kimbrough, Jr., and Carlton R. Young. *Psalms for Praise and Worship: A Complete Liturgical Psalter.* Nashville: Abingdon Press, 1992.

Inclusive-Language Psalms from an Inclusive-Language Lectionary. New York: Pilgrim Press, 1987.

Loh, I-to, ed. *Hymns from the Four Winds: A Collection of Asian American Hymns.* Nashville: Abingdon Press, 1983.

————, ed. *Sound the Bamboo: CCA Hymnal 1990.* Manila: Asia Institute for Liturgy and Music, 1990.

Lyke, James P., ed. *Lead Me, Guide Me.* Chicago: GIA Publications, 1987.

Marshall, Jane. *Grace, Noted.* Compiled and edited by Rosemary Heffley. Carol Stream, Ill.: Hope Publishing, 1992.

Martinez, Raquel Mora, ed. *Mil Voces para Celebrar: Himnario Metodista.* Nashville: United Methodist Publishing House, 1996.

Murray, Shirley Erena. *Every Day in Your Spirit: New Hymns Written between 1992 and 1996.* Carol Stream, Ill.: Hope Publishing, 1996.

————. *In Every Corner Sing: The Hymns of Shirley Erena Murray.* Carol Stream, Ill.: Hope Publishing, 1992.

Troeger, Thomas H. with Carol Doran. *New Hymns for the Lectionary: To Glorify the Maker's Name.* New York: Oxford University Press, 1986.

————. *New Hymns for the Life of the Church: To Make Our Prayer and Music One.* New York: Oxford University Press, 1992.

Turney, Kelly, ed. *Shaping Sanctuary: Proclaiming God's Grace in an Inclusive Church.* Chicago: Reconciling Congregations Program, 2000.

Webber, Robert, et al. *Renew! Songs and Hymns for Blended Worship.* Carol Stream, Ill.: Hope Publishing, 1995.

Winter, Miriam Therese. *Songlines: Hymns, Songs, Rounds, and Refrains for Prayer and Praise.* New York: Crossroad Publishing, 1996.

With One Voice: A Lutheran Resource for Worship. Minneapolis: Augsburg Fortress, 1995.

Wren, Brian. *Bring Many Names.* Carol Stream, Ill.: Hope Publishing, 1989.

————. *Faith Looking Forward: The Hymns & Songs of Brian Wren with Many Tunes by Peter Cutts.* Carol Stream, Ill.: Hope Publishing, 1983.

————. *Faith Renewed.* Carol Stream, Ill.: Hope Publishing, 1995.

————. *New Beginnings: 30 New Hymns for the 90's.* Carol Stream, Ill.: Hope Publishing, 1993.

————. *Piece Together Praise: A Theological Journey.* Carol Stream, Ill.: Hope Publishing, 1996.

————. *Praising a Mystery: 30 New Hymns by Brian Wren.* Carol Stream, Ill.: Hope Publishing, 1986.

Works Cited in This Book

Bell, John L., ed. *Common Ground: A Song Book for All the Churches.* Edinburgh: Saint Andrew Press, 1998.

————. *Sent by the Lord: Songs of the World Church.* Vol. 2. Chicago: GIA Publications, 1992.

Berthier, Jacques. *Songs & Prayers from Taizé.* Chicago: GIA Publications, 1991.

Buechner, Frederick. *Wishful Thinking: A Seeker's ABC.* San Francisco: HarperSanFrancisco, 1993.

Davies, J. G., ed. *The New Westminster Dictionary of Liturgy and Worship.* Philadephia: Westminster Press, 1986.

Davis, Noel. *Love Finds a Way.* New South Wales: Shekinah Creative Center, 2000.

De Bono, Edward. *New Think: The Use of Lateral Thinking in the Generation of New Ideas.* New York: Avon Books, 1971.

Doran, Carol and Thomas H. Troeger. *Trouble at the Table: Gathering the Tribes for Worship.* Nashville: Abingdon Press, 1992.

Driver, Tom F. *Liberating Rites: Understanding the Transformative Power of Ritual.* Boulder: Westview Press, 1997.

Duck, Ruth C. *Finding Words for Worship: a Guide for Leaders.* Louisville, Ky.: Westminster/John Knox Press, 1995.

The Faith We Sing. Nashville: Abingdon Press, 2000.

Fink, Peter E., ed. *The New Dictionary of Sacramental Worship.* Collegeville: Liturgical Press, 1990.

Gardner, Howard. *Frames of Mind: The Theory of Multiple Intelligences.* New York: BasicBooks, 1993.

Grudin, Robert. *The Grace of Great Things: Creativity and Innovation.* Boston: Mariner, 1997.

Hahn, C. Michael. *Halle, Halle: We Sing the World Round: Songs from the World Church for Children, Youth, and Congregation.* Garland: Choristers Guild, 1999.

Hickman, Hoyt L., Don E. Saliers, Laurence Hull Stookey, and James F. White. *The New Handbook of the Christian Year.* Nashville: Abingdon Press, 1992.

Kimbrough, S T, Jr., ed. *Global Praise 1 and 2.* New York: GBGMusik, 1996, 2000.

McFee, Marcia. *Creating a Dance for Worship.* Alameda, Calif.: Peace by Peace Productions, 1995.

————. *Kinetic Meditations: Four Prayers for the Morning.* Alameda, Calif.: Peace by Peace Productions, 1998. Videocassette.

Saliers, Don E. *Worship Come to Its Senses.* Nashville: Abingdon Press, 1996.

Schneider, Pat. *The Writer As an Artist: A New Approach to Writing Alone and with Others.* Los Angeles: Lowell House, 1993.

Stookey, Laurence Hull. *Let the Whole Church Say Amen! A Guide for Those Who Pray in Public.* Nashville: Abingdon Press, 2001.

Webber, Robert, et al. *Renew! Songs and Hymns for Blended Worship.* Carol Stream, Ill.: Hope Publishing, 1995.

White, James F. *A Brief History of Christian Worship.* Nashville: Abingdon Press, 1993.